An Intelligent Visitor's Guide to the Irish

Breda Dunne

THE MERCIER PRESS

The Mercier Press, 4 Bridge Street, Cork
24 Lower Abbey Street, Dublin 1

British Library Cataloguing in Publication Data
Dunne, Breda
  An intelligent visitor's guide to the Irish
  1. Ireland (Republic). Business Practices
  I. Title
  650. 09417

  ISBN 0-85342-937-5

For Aonraid and Owen

Typeset by Seton Graphics, Bantry, Ireland.
Printed in the Republic of Ireland by Leinster Leader, Naas, Co. Kildare.

Contents

Introduction

I have often felt sorry for the visitor in our midst, the tourist or business person who, in a very short period of time, has to get to know us Irish well enough so as to be able to get the most from his/her holiday here or to conduct business effectively with us. And so I decided to write this book.

Now, if you are a visitor about to read it, it is necessary to tell you right away that in reading it you probably won't get an answer to all the questions you have about the Irish. But, hopefully, it will steer you in the direction of the more critical features to look out for while among us. And if after you have managed to get to know us a little, your curiosity has been aroused and you would like to become better acquainted with us as a people, then the bibliography given at the end of the book may help you in this task.

It is also probably desirable at the very beginning to alert you to the fact that the Irish are a difficult people to understand. We Irish still have great difficulty trying to figure ourselves out as a people, and what it is that makes us what we are. And the fact that we have spent so much time on this task over the years, and still think it necessary to continue to devote so much time and effort to pondering over the issue, shows just how complicated it really is!

The reason why the Irish are difficult to understand lies in the contradictions that exist within the Irish personality. The Irish are riddled with contradictory characteristics. We are a highly spiritual and imaginative people with a great love of dreams, visions and language which helps us express our own visions and ideals. We can get carried away by a metaphor, a poem or an idea which has been 'packaged' in emotional language — the very word 'nation' can bring tears to our eyes. Yet we are also the most down-to-earth, dull, soulless people one could ever come across, who would think nothing of knocking down or blowing up parts of our national heritage. Since we achieved political independence in 1922 we have created a rather boring society, with few aspirations. We just plod along with our eyes to the ground concerned only with eeking out a living for ourselves, with keeping 'body and soul together'.

But just when you have made up your mind about us and decided that we are essentially plodders and survivors you will discover that we are not good at this task. Contrary to what one might expect, we are not particularly good survivors. We are not practical or realistic enough. Instead of rationally trying to see and deal with problems we are much more likely to pretend they are not there, and to escape into an imaginary realm of great hope and optimism.

Dealing with the Irish is often very confusing. It is somewhat like dealing with a Jeckyll and Hyde type of character — one minute we present one image of ourselves and the next a very different one seems to emerge. Take the case of the Irish farmer who can be brought to the point of weeping when singing ballads and telling stories about the old Celtic ways of his forefathers, yet will think nothing of knocking down Celtic ruins so that he can widen the gate for the cattle. As a result of his ill thoughtout and hasty activities he may find himself in trouble with conservation authorities and groups. But once finding himself in trouble he is likely to be astute and shrewd enough politically to know how to go about getting himself out of the 'pickle'. How do you begin to understand someone like this, who appears to have so many different characteristics, who seems to be such a contradiction — romantic yet soulless; a fool yet no fool; rash and lacking in judgement, yet astute and cunning when cornered?

We Irish wonder and puzzle over this split personality which we seem to have. A possible explanation for it is that it has come about as a result of the effects of our history on our natural personality. Our natural disposition, from what

is known about our Celtic ancestors, would appear to be
that of a spiritual, imaginative, reckless, flamboyant people,
who were not very practical or industrious in the modern
sense of the word. Now this group of spirited people
underwent a traumatic experience, extending over many
centuries, when they were reduced to the status of landless,
persecuted and poverty-stricken peasants, and at their
lowest point, in their darkest hour, over one million died
from hunger and famine in the mid-nineteenth century. This
whole experience left its impact on us. For centuries our
ancestors were forced to toil and slave with their backs to
the wall just in order to survive, to cope with the dull yet
vital task of scraping out a living. It dampened their innate
spirited disposition yet did not totally extinguish the spark
or fire of their natural personality. Instead the two elements
continued to exist side by side in an uneasy relationship
with each other. Thus the Irish developed as a people who
are difficult to understand and certainly hard to predict.

And just as our ancestors colonial experiences affected
yet did not erase their natural disposition, so also the
modern world, with its philosophy and way of life, has
affected but has not eroded, or in any real sense super-
seded our traditional philosophy and way of life. Here
again the Irish remain caught between two quite different
'forces' — overtly presenting most of the time a modern
image, yet every so often shocking, not only foreigners, but
even ourselves, by the continuing power and strength of
many of our traditional beliefs and values.

In the chapters that follow the main or dominant individual features or characteristics of the Irish are considered. It
is desirable for the foreigner to appreciate these and the
complexity of the Irish personality. It is not simple and
straightforward and it is very easy for him to misjudge it.
An Irish person who projects a genuine 'hail-fellow-well-
met' outlook, may also have beneath that jovial exterior a
sad pessimistic attitude which is just as real. Those foreigners
who put a high value and importance on order, constancy

and consistency in life, including social life, will find the Irish and Irish society difficult to take. Far better for this kind of foreigner, in the interests of his health and sanity, not to expect to satisfy these values while in Irish society. He will be much happier and certainly less frustrated if he takes the Irish as he finds them. He should not question too much or too closely the inconsistencies in attitudes, views and behaviour, nor dwell too much on the fact that what we say and do may differ from one day to the next, or even from one minute to the next!

In writing a book about your own people it is probably prudent to lay your cards on the table and to divulge your personal views and judgements on your subject matter, to give some idea of whether you like or dislike them as a people and whether you want to be associated with them or not. Apart from alerting the reader to possible conscious or unconscious biases in the work, it satisfies the need many readers have to know your assessment of the people you are writing about.

So, having this need in mind, I bear my soul!

The first thing to say is I am Irish and very proud of my national identity. But, hopefully, this fact does not cause me to lose my perspective when critically looking at the Irish as a people. I recognise and accept that like every other race we have features that would generally be considered positive and others that would probably be widely regarded as negative. I love the positive features and hope we can hold on to them. I worry about the negative ones and have spent many years working to try and eliminate a number of these.

In my view, the most positive attribute of the Irish is definitely our complex or multi-dimensional world view or philosophy of life and living. We like material goods as much as the next group of people. Nevertheless the Irish do not live in the narrow, confined materialist world of many modern societies, where all of life and living is reduced to the satisfaction of material needs and desires. We do not have a society in which the individual's prime role in life is that of being a producer and consumer of goods and services. The Irish philosophy of life is much broader. The spiritual nature and existence of the individual is generally accepted. Values other than material-related ones have a high value and importance. Friendship, companionship, 'wasting time' and many other non-material qualities and activities are considered to be very important within Irish society. The Irish talk less about human self-realisation than some other groups, yet are much more committed believers and practitioners of this ideal than those who talk a lot about it. Our philosophy is very much in line with that of modern philosophers and psychologists, such as Abraham Maslow. He maintains that the true nature of the human is one which requires and needs spiritual as well as material values.

It is often only when the Irish person has lived and worked outside Ireland for a time that he/she begins to appreciate the extent to which 'living' in the full and total human sense is important to the Irish. The simple or one-dimensional materialistic view of life and living that exists in many other modern societies can be very unfulfilling for the Irish person. When we find ourselves in situations like this we often begin to appreciate more fully the true meaning of modern clichés such as the 'quality of life'. We realise that this encompasses not just the number of television sets you have, or even the state of the environment surrounding you, but also, and even more importantly, the quality of one's social and human life.

And now to the other side — the weaknesses. The Irish would be a much more attractive people if we could manage to rid ourselves of the 'cute peasant' features which we developed in our efforts to survive in the past. The selfish non-enlightened self-interest which we manifest towards each other and our extreme conservatism are not endearing or desirable features.

However our biggest weakness and problem as I see it, is, our generally poor performance in managing ourselves and in being able to survive effectively in the modern world. Our lack of self-confidence and our poor leadership ability don't help in this respect. But our most serious drawback appears to be the poor 'fit' that seems to exist between us and what is required for good organisational functioning. This is a critical weakness in a world where organisations, both public and private, are the main forces within society.

The main reason for our problem is quite simply that we are not sufficiently one-dimensional to make good organisation people. The very qualities that are most attractive about us — our complex view of life and how to live it to the full — are drawbacks in terms of our effective functioning and survival within organisations. A group of people who don't see material ends and objectives as all there is to life; who don't see work as the only, or even the most fulfilling, activity in life; who don't see material achievement and success as the main indicators of a person's worth within society may have difficulty in the modern world. They may be less well-suited to organisational life, than a group for whom material-related values are the only set of values that really matter.

I am in no doubt that we Irish have a problem in terms of making our way in the world. We need to become better workers and managers. But, hopefully, we can achieve this without losing our 'soul' or spirit. The problem we face is that we need to become sufficiently one-dimensional in our economic and working lives so that we can survive effectively, but at the same time need to be watchful lest we undergo a conversion from our traditional view of life and living to the simple materialist philosophy underlying organisation and management thinking. The difficult task that faces us is to learn to live a life devoted to objectives, targets, rationality, discipline, achievement, success, etc., from 9 o'clock to 5 o'clock as it were, and still preserve our much richer traditional philosophy and way of life. While we have not consciously acknowledged or faced up to our dilemma in trying to balance those two sets of values we often give evidence that deep down we are aware of our problem. In fact, one often senses that this not very well articulated problem which lies around our collective subconscious adds yet another layer of complexity to our already complex and complicated national personality. Our difficulty is that we want the fruits of the material society, yet, at the same time, we don't want to become, in the full sense, a materialist society.

I suppose if I had to state in one word what I most like about my people, it is our complexity. It is these contradictions and conflicts which give us our truly distinctive collective character and personality. And now that I've given you my assessment of the Irish, I'll leave you to decide for yourself what you think of us.

But, before I end, a word to the Irish readers who may be furtively peeping through these pages, curious to find out what is being said about them to outsiders. Go on — have a good look and think about the points made — for I don't think that as a people we look at ourselves sufficiently critically. Over the years many good critics, such as Seán O'Faoláin, Charles McCarthy and Joseph Lee, have given us food for thought about ourselves, but we shouldn't rely exclusively on the formal critic to help us see and understand ourselves better. Many more of us ordinary characters need to take on the job as well. But, of course, there is little point in increasing our understanding of ourselves if we are not prepared to face up to the reality that is revealed. While some of our characteristics may be ones that we like and would like to retain, we may need to accept that others are not helping us in terms of surviving in the modern world. The task that we face is to get to know ourselves well enough to be able to decide on which features of our collective personality we should or can afford to hold on to, and those which need to be changed or modified in the interest of our survival.

CHAPTER 1

The Residue of Colonialism

Eight hundred years of British colonial rule has left its mark on the Irish. When the British withdrew in 1922 they left behind them more than their institutions and traditions. They also left behind a people with a wide range of colonially induced attitudes and values, which were deeply imbedded in their consciousness and which we have found difficult to shake off. Some of these attitudes and values were developed for purposes of physical as well as psychological survival during colonial rule. Significant among these was and is the Irish attitude to law and order and to authority.

Other attitudes and characteristics emerged as a result of the conditions in which our Irish ancestors found themselves. They were reduced to the status of a poverty-stricken persecuted people, without a leadership class. In the absence of a natural class of leaders a spirit of egalitarianism developed. The idea thus evolved that nobody had any reason to feel better than anyone else. Our ancestors were probably no different from any other group, who at a time in their history suffered the degradation of colonialism.

When the coloniser had gone, and all we were left with were the remnants of colonial institutions, traditions and language, we began to wonder who we actually were — perhaps we were only a second-class people after all? The whole colonial episode has left scars on the Irish pysche. It has caused us doubts about our national identity. At times our quest for this identity seems to border on the obsessional, and appears to block out the wider issues and problems of our relationship with the world outside our own little island.

But despite all our efforts to work out who we are, we can give the impression of not being really interested in coming to grips with the question and with facing up to the answer that is likely to emerge. A realistic consideration of ourselves and our past reveals a lot that is different from popularly held views about us. These views depict us as a Gaelic people who suffered under colonial rule, particularly in the last 300 years, and who emerged in the end as a Gaelic people, who had, however, been contaminated by English culture and who consequently needed to go back to our own native culture and way of life. We needed to become in the words of one of our ballads 'a nation once again'.

The reality is however that by the end of the colonial period the Irish were no longer in any real sense the Gaelic people we had been 300 years before. Neither genetically nor culturally were we the Gaels of the seventeenth century. Intermarriage during the intervening centuries with English and Scottish planters, soldiers and other non-Irish who found themselves on this island had certainly introduced a lot of English and Scottish blood into the old Gaelic and Norman-Gaelic families. The old Gaelic culture had taken a hammering from the English culture which by the end of the nineteenth century had managed to establish a firm hold among the Gaelic-Irish. But even though our ancestors had adopted the English language and many aspects of English culture they still remained a very distinct people and their culture remained in many critical areas and aspects Gaelic in nature. One could say that what had taken place over the centuries was the gradual fusion of two groups of people and two cultures. The end result was a 'new' people and a 'new' culture — a 'new' Anglicised Gaelic people and culture — neither pure Gaelic or English, but a unique blend of the two.

Many influential leaders within post-independence society did not accept this reality. And many still continue to operate on the basis of the Irish being a Gaelic people, still maintaining that we need to go back to our old Gaelic culture and way of life. When viewed against this background is it any wonder that we Irish are a bit confused about our identity! We have been 'fed' an image of ourselves based on a myth which deep down we know is not true but which we have done very little to repudiate.

Colonialism was the initial problem and it certainly left some negative scars on the Irish personality. But the present problem is to get the Irish to face up to some of the real effects or outcomes of the colonial period rather than merely the effects or consequences which we like to attribute to it.

Little Regard for Law, Order and Authority

The Irish have the reputation, particularly among their ex-colonial masters, of being a lawless people, of not having a great love or regard for the law of the land. 'The Celts,' wrote Matthew Arnold, the English poet and writer, in the late nineteenth century, 'are undisciplinable, anarchical and turbulent of nature.'[1] His view would reflect that of many British people who have had contact with the Irish. But unlike many other weaknesses or vices which the British are likely to ascribe to us, this characteristic would probably be acknowledged by the Irish as well. We know that we are a fairly lawless kind of people, and we don't need studies to prove it either to ourselves or to others. All the observer has to do is look around to see the evidence. It is everywhere — little observance of traffic-lights by either motorists or pedestrians; cars 'abandoned' on yellow lines; drinking in bars and lounges after official closing-time. One is regularly brought back to the conclusion that the Irish are a people not too much caught up in the observance of the law.

And it's not just the behaviour of the people which shows a disregard and disrespect for the law, but our attitudes also reflect this outlook. Some authority figures, or specifically authority figures who are involved in the law-making administration processes within the state — members of our Dáil, government, judges, police, etc. are held in fairly low esteem. They are often seen by the ordinary citizen as being 'out for themselves' or 'on the make'. It would be very difficult to convince the citizen that these public servants might have a sense of public duty or responsibility, and want to contribute their talents towards the improvement of Irish society. The expression of such a view would bring howls of laughter from the ordinary citizen!

This generally held view of public servants is in sharp contrast however to the view the Irish hold in relation to other authority figures, most strikingly Church leaders. The Church, or more specifically the Catholic Church, has traditionally occupied a very powerful and respected position in Irish society, and this continues right up to the present day. The Church speaks with authority, and this authority is recognised and respected by a great majority of the Irish people, even though it is less likely to go unquestioned today than it did in the past. Up to more recent times the Church was seen by many as passing on some of its authority to others within society, particularly teachers. They were given some of this 'referred' authority because of the important task they had, as seen in the eyes of the Church, of moulding their young students into good Catholics. However, in more recent years trade unionism within the teaching profession has done much to down-grade the high esteem and respect in which teachers were once held.

There seems to be little dispute about the fact that the Irish have little respect for the law or for anyone with anything to do with it. The reasons why this is so are less obvious. We are told by historians that our distant ancestors, the Celts, were a flamboyant people, who were not easy to govern or control. Despite the mixture of bloods which make up the Irish nation of today, perhaps these distinguishing characteristics of the Celts still predominate? A more likely explanation in the opinion of many, however, is our British colonial background.

The Irish never respected or accepted British law. Unlike our old code of laws — the Brehon Laws — it did not embody our ancestors' values. It was always seen as an alien set of laws that enshrined a foreign way of life. From the seventeenth century on, it included legislation which was deliberately intended to penalise Irish Catholics because of their religion. Consequently, it is not difficult to understand the dislike which the Irish had for the British law and its agents, and why it was felt that justice could not be received from this foreign legal system.

There is no disputing the degree of lawlessness which existed in Ireland during British Rule. One of the most notable examples of this is in the picture historians have given us of the Irish faction fighters of the nineteenth century. These fighting groups, comprised of members of specific families or clans, came together and fought each other in very bloody encounters. While in some cases they fought to settle family feuds, in many other cases they fought as one historian has put it, 'for the sheer love of fighting.'[2]

This phenomenon was totally incomprehensible to the British at the time. In the 1830s a travel writer commented disbelievingly on the complete lack of motive in these fights. 'The English murder is perpetrated by some ruffian for the sake of gain, but the Irish homicide is committed for no reason at all.'[3] But perhaps these fights had a more deep-seated cause or motivation than was apparent to the English commentator? Maybe they were attempts to retain some spirit and dignity, an escape from the trials and tribulations of the inferior status of the natives, and an act of defiance towards the despised authorities?

But it wasn't only in fighting and in causing disturbances of the peace that the Irish showed non-acceptance and disrespect for English law. It was also shown in the court-room. Here the struggle was between English law and Irish ingenuity. In nineteenth century law-courts in Ireland the art of perjury reached, as one commentator has put it, 'hither to undreamed of heights'.[4] Indeed he adds that it was organised into something like a science, and certain types of defence came to be recognised by the names of the counties in which they had been perfected. The whole objective of the Irish witness was to 'get round the law'. By a combination of irrelevant information and feigning misunderstanding, the witness hoped he would confuse rather than clarify the facts sought of him, and exasperate the court into finishing with him before he had 'given away' anything that might assist the authorities.

But while it may be easy enough to comprehend why our ancestors thought and acted as they did when under foreign laws, the question could reasonably be asked as to why the situation did not change after the establishment of our own state. Although nobody has yet arrived at a satisfactory answer to this question, we can speculate on a few possible reasons. It is conceivable that the English laws and legal system retained after independence just don't suit us as a people, irrespective of who administers them. Then again, maybe writers such as Arnold were not too far wrong and the Irish do indeed have a tendency towards an anarchic disposition, a characteristic which has been aggravated by colonial experiences.

Lack of Leadership and a Spirit of Egalitarianism

The Irish have no native leadership class — a class of people who for many generations by virtue of their up-bringing and education have seen themselves as the national guardians of the public realm and its traditions. The Irish nobility were forced to leave the country during the seventeenth and eighteenth centuries and the Anglo-Irish aristocracy, or ruling-class, who took their place were never accepted by the native Irish. Some members of that class, such as Charles Stewart Parnell, a leading parliamentary agitator for Home Rule in the nineteenth century, did become powerful and influential figures among the native Irish. However, as a class, the efforts of the Anglo-Irish to exercise leadership over the people never fully succeeded, even when some of its members tried to lead a cultural revolution to restore the old Gaelic culture within Irish society, and to fuse it with their own Anglo-Irish culture. No real spirit of communion existed between the natives and this colonial group, with its English accent, manner and loyalties, and its Protestant faith.

After the establishment of the Free State the Irish were prepared to grant the defeated Anglo-Irish caste — the 'Horse Protestants' as they were called — the right to remain on in Ireland, to recognise their property and institutional rights, but that was the limit of it. It was the native Irish who were to exercise the real power in the new state, and it was this culture that was to dominate economic, social and cultural life.

With the emergence of the new state positions of power and influence in all walks of public life changed hands. Individuals with a much different background took over the reins of power and leadership. But it is one thing to take over a position of leadership and quite another to exercise real leadership. Many critics maintain that the new men did not provide the leadership required by the situation, and that as a result many of the causes for the failings and inadequacies within Irish society today began to develop. Their failure was that they did very little to develop and build a really definitive Irish state and society. They took over and continued to maintain the institutions of state they had inherited, the civil service, army, judiciary etc., but did little to assess and possibly change these, so that they would more effectively meet the specific needs of Irish society.

They also failed to grapple in a realistic way with the problem of developing our distinct cultural identity. Instead we have remained very firmly within the orbit of British culture. We speak English and are content to lead a way of life that is no different, in any significant way, from that lived by the people across the Irish Sea.

One of the biggest difficulties that all new states face emerging from colonial rule, is a shortage of able people. They have too few people with leadership qualities and skills, who are capable of taking over the key positions within the society. So perhaps the initial scarcity of leadership talent after 1922 is understandable. However it is taking a long time to rectify the situation. After more than 60 years of Irish self-rule there is still strong evidence to suggest that Irish society continues to suffer from poor leadership in key areas of public life.

The only group of people who have exercised any real leadership since the foundation of the state are Catholic Church leaders. One could say that this group is the closest the Irish have to a national leadership class — a group recognised and accepted by the public as the social, economic and political leaders of the country. Over the years they have constantly been in the background, ensuring that the direction Irish society is taking is one that is acceptable to them. And when it has seemed to them to be going off course, they have not been afraid to speak out and give their critical opinions. In recent years they have spoken out on abortion and divorce and caused much anger and resentment among Irish liberals. Now they are speaking out against the selfish, uncaring nature of Irish society, a community where poverty is on the increase and the better off just don't seem to care. They have had, and continue to have, a vision of the kind of society they want for the Irish, and they have always been prepared to use their power and influence in efforts to bring about this society.

On the other hand, Dáil (parliamentary) representatives are regularly criticised in relation to the leadership, or lack of it, which they are perceived to give, and much of this criticism is probably justified. Most representatives are extremely locally orientated. The extent to which they are genuinely concerned with national issues is a matter often speculated on. In addition, they see their roles as doing what the citizen wants of them, rather than providing leadership in any real sense. They spend a lot of their time working as a kind of consumer representative, sorting out problems individuals may be having with various public bodies. When not working on behalf of the individual citizen, they are pleading cases in the Dáil and elsewhere on behalf of specific groups within their constituencies. Nor does there appear to be any change taking place in how the public representative sees and carries out his role. One political commentator gave his verdict on the topic in the early 1980s and stated that the number of representatives and candidates for election 'willing to pander to localism is possibly still on the increase'.[5]

The electoral system of proportional representation is often cited as a major cause of this phenomenon. After all, the representative has to ensure that he looks after the needs of the local electorate better than any other representative, even one from his own party, so as to ensure that he gets their vote at the next election. Be that as it may, many Irish would acknowledge that a national parliament made up of local consumer representatives, with little or no national perspectives or concerns, leaves a big gap or void in the community in terms of national leadership.

The senior civil servant, also, often comes under attack for his lack of vision and leadership. Like the public representative, he hasn't shown any great desire to lead the community in any special direction. Instead he appears to be happy to let it just plod at its own pace in whatever direction it appears to want to go. He sees his main job as one of protecting his minister, and towards this end spends most of his time and effort attending to all matters, both major and minor, that might, if not sorted out by him, cause embarrassment to the minister. Consequently, similar to the representative, he often hasn't much time left over for the bigger national issues.

A factor which in the past has been seen as possibly contributing to lack of leadership was educational background. Unlike the senior civil servants of pre-independent Ireland, and senior civil servants in Britain and many other European countries, the Irish civil servants often had a fairly narrow education. For example as late as 1963 over 60 per cent of top civil servants'positions were held by people who had entered the civil service straight from secondary school. But perhaps more important than the level of formal education which this leadership group had, was the nature of this education. In many cases it was received at Catholic Christian Brothers' schools. It was a fairly limited type of education, where the concentration was on preparing boys for examinations with a comparative neglect of non-academic or extra-curricular activities. The outcome was that it resulted in individuals reaching influential positions within the civil service without having the basic attributes, qualities or skills necessary for leadership. One commentator put it this way 'they are little prone to speculate broadly or to reflect on long-term ends or cultural values. They have restricted horizons and are likely to accept "the system" with little question.'[6]

The number of senior civil servants with university education is greater today than in the 1960s, but whether today's top bureaucrats are any more reflective or broader in their horizons than their predecessors is open to question. The situation still exists that many senior civil servants, who should see themselves as leaders in society, are just as likely to see themselves as workers within a bureaucracy. They are satisfied to punch in their hours, do what they think the minister wants them to do, and call on their trade union if they feel aggrieved with their conditions of service.

The Irish would definitely like more and better leadership from those in key public positions within the community. However the one thing we do not want is the re-emergence of an elite establishment class similar to the pre-1922 British one, except this time it would be home-grown — a class which would see itself as removed from, and above, the ordinary average citizen. For one quality that most Irish people like about our society, despite its many negative features, is the general spirit of egalitarianism which pervades it. Irish society is not by any means an egalitarian society in a real sense. There are significant social and economic divisions within society. However individuals generally feel a sense of being equal to others as human beings. The great distance between individuals of different socio-economic classes, often found in other societies, such as in Britain or France, does not exist to any great extent in Ireland. Irish society does not contain a group of people with a naturally condescending attitude towards others whom they genuinely consider to be their inferior.

This lack of a significant class-distinction is reflected in the informality which is characteristic of our personal dealings with each other. First names are generally used after very short acquaintance, and the use of more formal titles could in many cases be seen as pretentious. Our general spirit or air of egalitarianism contributes to making us an open, friendly and hospitable people, who find it easy to relate to others irrespective of class or nationality. This capacity to relate easily to a wide range of people is a characteristic which we have found to be a marketable commodity. Our non-class consciousness and open friendly disposition has been, and will continue to be, one of our strongest positive features in terms of business. Our ability to be easily accepted by foreigners, and to relate effectively to them on a one-to-one personal basis gives us a strong card which we are able to play in the international business game.

Problems of Identity

Colonialism caused the Irish personality to become unsure about its distinctiveness. This view and sentiment is one held by many Irish who consciously think about the issue of Irish identity. But it is important to state that this 'thinking' group is only a very small minority of the population. Most of the ordinary citizens have no conscious concerns or thoughts about the matter. This does not mean, however, that subconscious views and beliefs are not held, and that these in many cases imply a view of the Irish as being not quite as 'good' as some other nationalities. It is relatively easy to see what gave rise to the problem and to see the manifestations of it in Irish society today. However it appears to be proving quite difficult to overcome.

In 1922 part of Ireland got official independence from Britain. But many would question the extent to which we became really independent. As previously stated we continued to remain very closely tied to the British world. Our political and legal institutions were still based on British models; we spoke their language. A minority within the new state — the Anglo-Irish — were proud of their British heritage and ties and wanted their culture to be recognised. In terms of economics Britain remained our major trading partner. When it comes to assessing why the Irish didn't break out of the old British mould and seek to establish our own truly independent existence, views differ and commentators apportion disparate amounts of blame to different individuals and groups. Some place the primary blame on the ordinary citizens. We failed to respond or show any real interest in the efforts being made to restore the Irish language and Gaelic culture. We lacked the vision and the will to continue the great nationalist revolution, in which the achievement of political independence was but one step along the way to the establishment of a brand new Gaelic society.

While there may be much truth in this assessment, some found it difficult not to conclude, having read the ideas and sentiments expressed by the leaders of the Gaelic Revival and nationalist revolutionary movements, that what was on offer was not a vision for real people to live in the present or for the future. Instead what some of these movements presented to the people of Ireland were 'the ghosts of dead men, insisting that the living abandon their daily lives and simplify themselves to the point of becoming agents of the dead.'[7] Their dream of Ireland was very suitable as the material for theatrical productions, which is to be expected, since many of the leaders in these movements were poets and playwrights. But it wasn't the kind of vision that the ordinary Irish person could relate to, or see as having any relevance to the way he wanted to live his life in the modern world.

Some would maintain that it is unfair to say that all the ideas presented were only appropriate for the theatre. There were also genuine attempts to bring about real change in Irish society by men such as James Connolly, who sought to establish a socialist political system in Ireland. The difficulty was, however, that irrespective of the content or worth of any of these plans, they were unlikely to grab the imagination of the mass of Irish people. For the Irish were a people less likely than most to go along with grand designs of abstract ideals and visions. Ideals, dogmas and doctrines, whether enshrined in bible, charter or proclamation, have always left us cold. Even the Christian Church found this to be the case. While we readily embraced Christianity it was the elements of spirituality within that religion that appealed to us, not the dogma or doctrine that went along with it. It was only in the nineteenth century that the Catholic Church succeeded in bringing us somewhat into line in relation to adhering to Christian beliefs and behaviour.

In our traditional Gaelic culture, inspiration and direction for living did not come from abstract ideals or visions. Instead, they came from stories, legends and history which were reinterpreted and reconstructed by different generations, and from adhering to codes of behaviour that reflected our traditional wise and understanding view of human nature. Our old Brehon Laws demonstrated a lot about us in relation to these qualities. They showed us to be a people who had a very down-to-earth commonsensical view of both the individual and society.

Our political leaders put forward the ideals we were to achieve and criticised us for the wrongs we had committed, in particular for abandoning our language and culture. But we didn't listen and they didn't succeed in their efforts, although they may have succeeded in damaging our self-confidence as a people. What we needed at this critical point in our history were leaders who understood us better. We required leaders who, instead of presenting us with nicely worded lofty visions and lectures, built our self-confidence and helped and coaxed us to take our eyes off the ground and do just a little bit of dreaming. But if revolutionary movements did not persuade or help us to do that little bit of dreaming and work out a programme for a new Ireland, neither did the new leaders of Irish society. Rather than innovate they became slavish imitators of British models. They stepped into the shoes of their ex-colonial masters and were content to continue on, as if nothing had happened, other than a change of leadership personnel.

Thus the matter was not resolved in the first decades of the new state, and consequently the debate and discussions on the need for the Irish to consciously set about recognising our distinct Irish identity is just as much in evidence, and as lively today, as it was in the 1920s and 1930s. Some claim that the restoration of the Irish language is essential if the Irish are to retain a national identity. Others claim that what is needed is a world image — a way of seeing and inter-preting the world from our own viewpoint and in our own terms. One writer put it this way, 'in business, science ... etc., the vast bulk of our thinking is derivative.'[8] What is needed is an Irish world image that would enable us to recognise our own way of seeing and doing things, which would do away with our need to slavishly imitate and copy the beliefs, values and activities of others.

It certainly appears that the Irish are only too willing to copy others in many areas and aspects of life — whether in relation to what policy to pursue in a certain area of govern-ment or what fashions to follow next autumn. We are reluctant to venture forward and make our own inde-pendent assessment or judgement in situations. Also it seems that this lack of confidence may be related to our weak sense of identity and uncertainty in relation to who or what we really are.

This problem of identity could be seen as initially stemming from the confusion-inducing myth that was developed and propagated at the foundation of the state. We were told we were really a Gaelic people and had a duty to recognise and develop a truly Gaelic society. When this myth was found inadequate by the majority of our people, those who thought further about the matter were left with the problem of trying to come to grips with who we really are. And since there is no doubting the similarities that exists between us and the people across the Irish Sea, it was probably natural that some might come to see themselves as West Britons.

But while on the surface there are many similarities between the Irish and the British the differences are in many crucial respects greater than the similarities. The Irish are, as I try to show in this book, a unique and very distinct race of people, whose collective personality, philosophy and way of life are very definitely unique creations. And the image that encapsulates the essence of our personality and philosophy of life and living is that of a complicated complex people, full of conflicts and contradictions.

The critical point is that we Irish have no need to have an identity crisis. Quite the reverse — very few groups of people are more distinct! We may have got off to a bad start at independence when we were given a bum steer by zealous but misguided leaders who tried to make us into a people and society we couldn't be. But it's about time we got back on the tracks again and woke up to the reality of our uniqueness. In order to find our special and peculiar qualities there is little point in studying ourselves at a superficial level. All that is visible there is the great similarity that exists between us and other 'moderns'. We generally look the same, act the same, and mouth the same ideas and sentiments as many other groups within modern western societies. But if we look below this superficial level, the myriad of unique features and characteristics will become apparent. The real Irish personality and philosophy will be there to see and observe.

By so doing, we may be able to rid ourselves of our national inferiority complex, a lack of confidence in our own judgement which results in a reluctance to make independent assessments about people or situations, without being given a nod or a sign by others. An example of this is the desirability, in fact almost necessity, for the Irish person with talent to be recognised by outsiders before he is likely to receive due recognition in his own society. Just as the real expert in our eyes is more often than not a foreigner, so also the Irish person who has made it abroad is seen as better and often preferable to the individual who has to rely exclusively on his Irish experience.

The feelings of inferiority which are far too common among the Irish and which are absolutely without foundation in objective terms, also show themselves in the tendency we have to be overly sensitive to criticism of all things Irish. This sensitivity seems to be more acute if the censure comes from an Irish emigrant or a foreigner. We are inclined to interpret criticism, even when it is intended and put forward in positive constructive terms, as efforts to 'put us down'. We don't see how we can learn from such fault-finding. Consequently not only do we not welcome unsolicited criticism but we will very rarely set out to solicit it. In our ordinary day-to-day dealings with each other we are often overly cautious in making complaints or criticising even when the situation warrants it — for example, when we receive poor quality in goods or services we don't want to be seen as trouble-makers or nuisances and our response to the situation is to complain behind the suppliers back but not to his face. The assumption is that the supplier is likely to interpret the complaint in a negative rather than a positive light, in a manner which is probably very similar to the way we would usually see and accept criticism.

The day the Irish actively look for feedback, even if it is critical, is the day the foreigner can begin to suspect that we may have developed our self-confidence — we will have the confidence to think and act in our own independent way, without constantly feeling the need to check out what others are doing, and to get their approval. We will welcome the views of others, but in the end have the confidence to do things our way. And when that day arrives, when the Irish get round to seeing and articulating their own distinct identity, the outcome should be beneficial not only to ourselves but also to others. For we will have much of significance to give to other people. Our people-centred view of the world and the many critical elements of pre-liberal materialism contained in our philosophy of life, are features that many modern western societies could usefully note and consider.

CHAPTER 2

A Nation of Peasants and Shopkeepers

The picture painted by writers and poets at the turn of this century was of the Irish peasant as a romantic figure. He was seen as fighting to retain his traditions and past civilisation intact from the onslaught of the modern industrial and utilitarian world — it was a glamorous, but very inaccurate portrait.

Yet the influence of poets such as W.B. Yeats, who did much to create this image, has been such, that this unreal image of the Irish peasant is widely regarded as being true. The vision projected by Yeats, Synge and others was of a dignified, rustic people, who exhibited the unspoiled simplicity of the essential Irish, and had endured the ravages of climate and oppression for many centuries. The rural lives they lived were seen as virtuous, as being an expression of the ancient Gaelic civilisation, which still remained uncontaminated by commercialism and progress.

Yeats and others were trying to project on to the Irish peasant the spiritual charm which had faded from the more industrialised countries of Europe. And while it was true that the Irish peasant still remained rustic and spiritual, this feature remained more by accident than by design. The Irish peasant was not fighting consciously to hold on to his old way of life. It just happened that the industrial revolution had not taken place in Irish society, so he had not had the opportunity to change this way of life.

However from the last quarter of the nineteenth century onwards, the Irish peasant was more concerned with progressing and improving his material lot than with remaining a historical specimen of an ancient civilisation, as Yeats and others would have liked him to have done. The reality is that from this time, the Irish peasant was intent on pulling himself up out of the abyss. He wanted to extract himself from the terrible life of poverty and deprivation which he had endured for many decades, and which came to a head during the years of the Great Famine of the 1840s. His ambition was to acquire as much land as he could, and to settle down to a good petit bourgeois type of existence.

During the last quarter of the century things began to look brighter for him. The dislocation in society in the period after the Great Famine helped those Irish who were fortunate enough to be still around — those who hadn't died or been forced to emigrate. Bit by bit significant numbers of the native Irish were renting or leasing ever increasing amounts of land, and through thrift and prudent actions, gradually the rural proletariat of the pre-Famine years was being transformed into a bourgeoisie.

It was during this period that many of the beliefs and values that still are dominant in Irish society began to emerge. As could be expected many of these beliefs and values were coloured by the background against which they developed. They reflected the thinking of a peasant society which was working very hard to become a petit bourgeois one. An individualistic view of the world was common — a belief that one had to look after oneself, and beware of others, all of whom were seen as potential rivals and threats.

Moreover there was no time for, or interest in 'airy-fairy' ideals. A down-to-earth practical approach to life and living was held to be much preferable and more desirable. And when you have had very little in the past, and now have something, it is reasonable that you should want to hold on to what you have acquired. So it is easy to understand why the Irish became very conservative and evolved a set of beliefs, values and attitudes which reflected this outlook. In particular there was a marked reluctance to take risks, even if in the long run they might have increased their chances of acquiring much greater wealth if they had done so.

A surface observation of the Irish and Irish society today would seem to indicate that the objective of becoming a modern bourgeois people and society has been more or less achieved. Our values and way of life appear to be similar to those of other western capitalist liberal democracies. But this surface likeness can be very misleading, for underneath the façade of modernity beats the heart of the traditional peasant. In many critical respects the Irish have never really entered the modern world. Many of the fundamental social and economic ideas that underpin modern western society have still not permeated Irish thinking. This is reflected not only in Irish social thinking, but also in the ordinary Irish business person's view and understanding of the fundamental principles of a capitalist system which can be unorthodox, to say the least. The Irish have been, and continue to be, happy and satisfied to take what they want from liberal bourgeois thinking and way of life. We certainly don't think that we have to accept everything — not even critical fundamental building blocks — in this philosophy. We are content to hammer together our own version of a bourgeois society, based mainly on traditional peasant values and beliefs.

The Individualist

The Irish farmer who was in the process of accumulating wealth — of adding field to field — saw all his neighbouring farmers as real or potential threats or enemies. After all, every field that they managed to acquire, meant that there was one less field there for him to go after. This unfriendly or unco-operative attitude towards his neighbours was not unique to the Irish peasant. Researchers have discovered similar attitudes and views to life in many other peasant cultures. They found that peasants view 'their social economic and natural resources — their total environment —

as one in which all the desired things in life, such as land, wealth, love, power etc., exist in finite quantities.'[1]

This view of the world influences social relations. It results in seeing others as rivals or threats, and being in constant competition for the scarce resources that are available. We believe that what others win we lose. We cannot accept a win-win type of outcome. And as might be expected our behaviour is affected by this view of life. It encourages us to engage in competitive power-orientated strategies, in which each player tries to minimise the gains of others — progress for the individual is seen as being a matter of getting ahead at the expense of someone else.

A win-lose way of perceiving life and others around one, has left its mark on the Irish character in general. It has encouraged the development of an individualistic personality, which views all the world as dangerous, and which is artful in the skills of getting the most it can out of any situation, even at the expense of others. Research carried out in recent years indicates that many Irish are still wary of other people and are still not greatly enthusiastic about the notion of co-operation with others to achieve something that would be mutually advantageous.[2]

It seems that there are two major obstacles when it comes to co-operating with others. Firstly, many still find it difficult to accept that it is possible that each party in a project or enterprise can benefit from the undertaking, in other words that everyone can be a winner. But perhaps the second obstacle may be even more difficult than this to overcome. It appears that many Irish will only co-operate when convinced that the advantage to others will not in any way, or to any degree, be greater than for themselves. We cannot bear the thought of one of our neighbours getting more out of a communal effort than ourselves. So it's not just a matter of all parties in a project or enterprise benefiting, but all must benefit in equal measure. Instances are regularly cited of community projects being aborted, because certain individuals involved were not convinced that they would get as much out of the project as their neighbours.

Moreover the individualistic phenomenon is not confined to the individual citizen and his dealings with others within his local community. The same narrow unenlightened self-interest is also apparent in the attitudes and behaviour of groups within the wider community. It is all too common for sections of society to pursue their own selfish ends to the detriment of the interests of others, for example, by taking strike action which causes enormous difficulties for their fellow citizens. Apart from the morality of their actions, they fail to see that these acts are often self-defeating. It seems that they are unable to perceive the interdependent nature of a modern society and consequently to appreciate the fact that in hurting others they are in the long run probably also doing damage to themselves. One writer described the battles between the different groups and sections within modern Irish society in blunt terms, when he said, 'the war today is not the war as Hobbes described it — of everyone against everyone, but of more and more groups that put themselves against the rest of society ... free from the trammels of collective morality and patriotic responsibility.'[3]

It is sad to look back at traditional Gaelic society where co-operation was seen to be of the highest importance. The ancient Brehon Laws clearly show the obligations that both the individual and the family had towards the wider community. The disintegration of that old society and the abandonment of its beliefs and values are to be regretted. Unfortunately, today, we Irish often give the impression that we don't understand or accept the idea of society as such. We don't acknowledge the notion of a general or common good which should be given priority over the good or interest of any individual or group within society. We don't even appear to be inclined towards accepting the much less lofty or less noble idea of enlightened self-interest. This utilitarian idea which forms the basis of the modern liberal society, holds that the enlightened individual helps the other person within society satisfy his wishes and desires, not for any more elevated reason than that the other person won't get in his way too much, or stop him in relation to meeting his needs and desires.

One often feels that the Irish have been so obsessed for the last one hundred years or so with creating a nation, that we have had little time for, or paid much attention to, creating or building a society. Without trying we have achieved the situation described by the British Prime Minister, Margaret Thatcher, who claims that 'there is no such thing as society, only individuals and families'. This philosophy which horrifies many British and Irish people because of the primitive individualistic society it advocates, is however, a fairly good and accurate description of the present existing state of Irish 'society'.

The Non-Idealist

The view of the Irish often held by foreigners, and indeed the image projected in many Irish history books, is of a people who are idealistic and revolutionary, who hold a vision of the world they want, and will stop at nothing to bring it about. In fact, nothing could be further from the truth. The reality is that for the last two centuries the Irish have shown themselves to be for the most part, one of the most down-to-earth, utilitarian people one could encounter. In the past we were certainly prepared to agitate, to use the rhetoric of idealism, and to engage in revolutionary tactics. But this was to gain what some really wanted — land — and once this was achieved, whatever little spark of idealism and vision was in us quickly went out.

The true model of the Irishman for anyone who wants to understand the Irish is Daniel O'Connell, not the great revolutionary heroes of Irish history such as Wolfe Tone or Pádraig Pearse. O'Connell was, as Seán O'Faoláin has said, a 'practical utilitarian, unsentimental' character who moulded the Irish peasants into a formidable political force in the late 1820s and using that force managed to gain for Catholics the right to be elected to the parliament at Westminster.[4] His major contribution to the Irish was not by way of giving our ancestors visions or dreams, but by helping them to develop the attitudes and skills they needed in order to survive as servants of Queen Victoria in the inhospitable world in which they found themselves. He showed them the power of the masses and taught them how to achieve political power through peaceful means. O'Faoláin thus believes him to be 'a far more appropriate model for twentieth century Ireland, than any figure drawn from the sagas or the mists of Celtic antiquity'.[5] O'Connell he maintains was 'Benthamite, English-speaking and philosophic about the loss of Gaelic...a figure to inspire a new Ireland'.[6]

Even while under British domination the Irish showed a practical utilitarian approach to life in order to survive. Nowhere is this more evident than in the approach to the Irish language. Even before the Famine F.S.L. Lyons, the historian, tells us the Irish people were well on their way 'to learning one painful but easily absorbed lesson — that the path to economic advancement whether in Ireland, Britain or America could only be trodden successfully by those who were prepared to exchange the language of the folk-museum for that of the market place.'[7] But, of course, not everyone was complacent about or indifferent to the loss of the Irish language. Some questioned the kind of survival we were going to have without it. One of the first to raise this issue was Thomas Davis, a contemporary of O'Connell, and one of the leaders of the revolutionary Young Ireland movement. Davis was in no doubt about the nature of the existence we would have without it. He tells us that 'to lose your native tongue and learn that of an alien is the worst badge of conquest — it is the chain of the soul. To have lost entirely the national language is death, the fetter has worn through.'[8]

However, little attention was paid to such views at the time. Practical survival, as we saw it, required abandoning the language of our forefathers. It also necessitated coming to terms with the government in Dublin. Alien though it was, it was a potential source of jobs and provided opportunities for advancement in life, and many young Irishmen took advantage of this. The army, police and public service provided many secure jobs, which enabled Irishmen carve out a decent life for themselves and their families.

Once political independence was achieved, and the land of Ireland was back with the people of Ireland — in particular with the farmers of Ireland — whatever bit of idealism that was around seems to have disappeared. The lack of vision, and dynamism, which the Irish have demonstrated since independence, has driven many of our cultural and political leaders almost to despair. The efforts of these leaders to get their fellow citizens to live their lives in their own way, and not to live the second-hand, hand-me-down life of somebody else, have fallen on, if not deaf, at least unreceptive ears. Douglas Hyde, one of the leaders of the Gaelic Revival Movement and the first president of the new state, found it difficult to work out the reasoning of the ordinary Irish person. 'It has always been curious to me,' he says, 'how the Irish continue to apparently hate the English, and at the same time continue to imitate them.... In the absence of developing our own identity, language and culture, we will become a nation of imitators, lost to the power of native initiative and alive only to second-hand ass'milation.'[9]

But despite the protests and efforts of a small minority within the new state to interest the ordinary Irish person in the challenge of creating a new society, one that would be uniquely Irish, the offer was not taken up. Those who would have been in the position, by virtue of their socio-economic standing in the new society, to assist in the innovating task were not interested. The newly emerging middle classes, among the farming population, in the towns and cities, were content, as one critic has said, 'to live a comfortable petit-bourgeois life that bore a closer relationship to the life of similarly placed people in Britain than to any vision of special destiny'.[10]

These characteristics of the Irish — our lack of vision, our unwillingness to have a dream of the society we want and to work to bring it about, the completely unromantic, down-to-earth approach to life — have continued to be a cause for disappointment among the more creative within society. During the period from the 1930s to the 1960s, no spark of creativity or innovativeness was apparent within Irish society, as many artists saw it. A socially conservative people were creating a society that was in the words of one commentator 'drab, respectable and dead'.[11]

Nor is Irish society today any different in its essentials from the society that has evolved over the last one hundred years. The Irish remain a non-ideological, non-philosophical or visionary people. Some would say that while down-to-earth and practical, we are not essentially realistic. At times we demonstrate a very uncertain grasp of the reality surrounding us. We are a bit like ostriches with our heads in the sand, not really aware of the reality of situations in which we find ourselves, even though these may be full of risks and dangers. One commentator has attributed this characteristic to our religious background, where we were taught to think beyond the immediate reality to the wider or larger reality of God's universe. The consequence of this far horizon training has been, he maintains, the development of a tendency to deny the reality of that which is closer to home, 'almost as if it were a matter of religious discipline to do so'.[12]

The absence of any dreams or visions in relation to an ideal future community is very apparent in Irish society. There is no national philosophy or purpose. A lot of talk and discussion takes place at the public level, but nothing seems to get translated into concrete ideas and programmes, that would aim to bring about a specific kind of community. The Irish are great talkers, but generally have little or no intention of doing anything to bring about the things or ideals we talk about. A very good example of this is the issue of the Irish language. Everyone thinks it's a good idea to have our own language, yet nobody, from members of government right down to the individual citizen, is keen to take action to back up his words. The only occasions when the Irish really get involved in an issue and when serious critical public discussion and debate occurs are when there is a likelihood of change taking place. Recent instances of this were the attempts to make divorce and abortion legal within the state.

Except when prompted by the possibility of change, we spend our time and energy getting on with the business of surviving, of doing the best we can to look after the day-to-day physical necessities of life. The sentiments expressed in a pop-song that was very popular in the country a few years ago, 'Help me to take one day at a time, sweet Jesus', probably sums up the Irish disposition to life and living better than anything Yeats or the romantic visionary poets and writers might have stated or hoped for.

The Conservative

The Irish are essentially a conservative people in relation to both the social and economic aspects of their lives. In the economic and business areas of life change is gradually taking place, but many would say that there is still too little taking place, affecting too few, and in many cases it is too late. Perhaps the degree and scope of change taking place in these spheres is indeed less than adequate. However, it is probably greater than that taking place in the social field — for in relation to social matters the majority of the Irish remain very definitely a conservative people.

Turning first to the social side of Irish society, an important point to make is that the beliefs, values and attitudes that are proving today to be very difficult to shift or change, are ones that are very deeply embedded in the Irish personality. Attitudes to the family, to marriage, to sex are all very firmly held, and are essential elements in a particular view, or philosophy of life. Many of these attitudes, and the behaviour patterns which they gave rise to, developed during the latter part of the nineteenth century and evolved to a large extent as a consequence of economic or material necessities.

One of the lessons which the peasant farmer had learned from the disaster of the Famine was the undesirability of dividing up his holding among his family on their marriage. The result of this action had been to create economically non-viable holdings that were too small to support a family adequately. Consequently the farmer of the late nineteenth century sought to keep his holding intact, and to pass it on as a single unit, to one of his sons, who would continue to carry on the family name. The social repercussions of this action were enormous. The absence of industrial development in rural areas and the limited educational opportunity for entry into the professions brought about severe social difficulties. They caused many of the remaining sons of the family, who would not inherit, and daughters for whom dowries would not be available, to have no option but to remain on as servants or labourers on the family farm or to get work in manual occupations locally, or else emigrate. Even sons and daughters lucky enough to have been chosen as successor to the farm, or given a dowry and married off to a local farmer, faced the prospect of a long wait before they achieved the status of farm-owner or wife. The Irish farmer was never in any hurry to pass over the reins of authority to his son, and the accumulation of a dowry took time.

The consequences of this calculated approach to farm succession were to seriously affect the marriage pattern within Irish society. Large numbers of men and women remained unmarried and even those who eventually did marry, married at a very late age. Statistics confirm this situation, for example, the 1926 Census revealed that in Ireland there was a larger proportion of unmarried persons of all ages than in any other country where records were kept. It is often said that the puritanical attitude of the Catholic Church in Ireland to sexual matters was in no small way a response to this potentially explosive situation! And many social historians now accept that the Church, in adopting this strict position, was merely reflecting the views of its members, who were resolutely determined to restrain sexuality in the interests of economic reality.

The price paid for this reality was high in social terms. Large numbers of Irish had no option but to emigrate, and many of those who remained had to make enormous sacrifices — no marriage or children for the unlucky, and late marriage for those who were fortunate. This prudent approach helped to create a society of bachelors and spinsters, a puritanical society of repressive sexual mores, a society where marriage was seen as a fulfilment of family obligations and responsibilities, rather than a personal right of the individual. There is no doubt about the continued influence of many of these beliefs and values on the Irish today. Despite the liberalisation of social beliefs and values which took place following the opening up of Irish society in the 1960s, the old beliefs and values still hold sway with many.

The referenda of recent years on abortion and divorce demonstrate clearly their continuing power and influence. They showed that the family, sexual propriety and property are still powerful elements within Irish society. In commenting on the Divorce Referendum of 1987 some observers maintained that the main reason why the Referendum was lost, and divorce not permitted, was not religious beliefs, or even the power of the Church in getting the people to vote against the motion, but rather reasons of property. They argued that many married women were worried about possible loss of their own property rights or those of their children, if a second marriage was allowed. The old peasant attitude of holding on to what you have got dies hard. Many felt, no doubt, that it was better to live a life of hell in a poor marriage than run the risk of losing the house or farm.

But it isn't only the memory of our impoverished past and the lessons we have learned from the past that has caused the Irish to be socially conservative. Our fundamental view of the nature of people has also inclined us in that direction. The Irish have never accepted one of the fundamental ideas in modern liberal thinking — the notion of social progress based on the perfectibility of the person. In this liberal thinking the modern enlightened individual is seen as being able, all on his own, without the help of society, to tread a very delicate tightrope. He is viewed as being capable of balancing two very desirable features, that of satisfying his own needs and desires and at the same time fulfilling his moral responsibilities.

Now the Irish, faithful to the traditional Catholic view have never accepted this enlightened outlook. With our 'fallen' view we are inclined to the belief that it would be expecting too much to be able to balance these two 'goods' without some aid or assistance from society. Consequently in our social thinking we accept the necessity for society to help the individual in this task by not allowing divorce, abortion, etc. Nor do we consider that this state of affairs is likely to change with time. After all, the modern individual is not any better, more moral or able to do without the help of society in helping him to live a good moral life, than the individual of 20, 50 or 100 years ago. So we do not see the extension of individual freedoms or liberties, for example legalising abortion or divorce, as social progress. Rather these extensions are seen as retrogressive steps. In sensitive social areas changes of the kind advocated by modern liberal thinkers are not considered by many Irish to be desirable either now or in the future. It would seem that in relation to the important social areas of sex, marriage and the family there is a happy and fortuitous concurrence between the way God sees things and the way the material-orientated Irish peasant wants things to be. Too much change might jeopardise the bit of property he/she has managed to acquire.

In relation to economic affairs and the Irish, because of the traditional and current importance of agriculture in Irish economic life, it may be appropriate to comment first on the farming sector in Irish business life. The critical actor in this whole story is of course the Irish farmer, and the first essential point to understand about him is how traditionally he has seen his farm and his business. The Irish peasant farmer had to fight hard for his piece of land, and when he got it, it became very much a part of him — it became part of his identity and a source of his self-esteem. The one thing it wasn't, to him, was a resource to be used.

Efforts have been made by numerous governments ever since the foundation of the state to make the farmer into a businessman, to get him to see farming as a commercial enterprise, but all of these efforts have had limited success. In 1927 the Agricultural Credit Corporation was set up to provide loans to farmers for productive purposes on reasonable terms. But the finances made available were not fully taken up. Even those farmers who took out loans, borrowed very small amounts. The reason for this could of course have been the small scale of Irish farming operations, but it could also reflect, as F.S.L. Lyons has put it, 'a deep seated reluctance on the part of the farmer to cumber himself with debt changes even in the interests of efficiency'.[13] It is also significant that there was a good deal of unpunctuality in the repayments of loans, leading sometimes, to actual default. The government's efforts to improve agricultural standards by providing the farmer with technical education and advice have not had the degree of success that many hoped for.

Ireland's entry into the EEC in 1973, naturally had a major impact on Irish agriculture. The Irish farmer benefited from the grants, levies and opportunities made available to him. But whether it has changed him in any significant way in his approach to farming and agriculture is another matter. It helped to bring into existence a corps of professional farmers, who are well-trained, and who operate in a professional business-like manner. The EEC greatly assisted in the development of this group, but outside this circle many of the old values, attitudes and behaviour patterns still remain. For the less progressive group of farmers the land continues to be seen as a hard-won possession — not a resource to be used economically to its optimum. They still remain reluctant to invest for productive purposes, to change from one kind of enterprise to another, or to use new methods and techniques of farming. They view with suspicion all these new ways, and wait apprehensively to see what happens to those who adopt them. And many are never more delighted or satisfied than when something goes wrong for someone who has tried to be innovative. The phrase 'sure I told you so' meaning, I knew you wouldn't succeed with that new idea, is one the progressive farmer has to be ready to hear from many 'knockers' all around him, when his efforts to improve his business occasionally backfire. In the Irish farming community it is still difficult for the go-ahead farmer to get praise, for at every corner there are scores around waiting to knock him.

Traditionally in Irish society being in business, which included trade and manufacturing, but did not include agriculture, was not very highly thought of. This attitude is not of course confined to the Irish. The business person has suffered from a low status in many societies other than Ireland. The most notable instance is Britain, where as late as 1962 an observer commented that 'nowhere else in the industrialised world are trade and manufacture regarded to such an extent as means to better things — to politics, land-ownership, to culture, to a position in the City'.[14]

Whether the Irish were tainted by this British view of business, which saw it as rather a distasteful way of making a living, or whether our attitudes were formed based on experiences in dealing with the native gombeen man is not clear. The gombeen man was the local businessman who was 'in to everything' — he ran the local stores, was the building contractor, funeral undertaker, etc. — and was often seen as a money-grabbing, dishonest, parasite within the local community. For whatever the reason the fact is that the businessman was held in low esteem, and business was not a profession that the average Irish mother wanted her son to pursue. Instead her ambition would likely be to have him go into the professions or into the civil service. A good respectable, secure, pensionable job was what every ambitious Irish youth and his mother wanted.

This traditional attitude towards business has very gradually begun to change. Major changes in the educational system in the 1960s and 1970s did much to publicly recognise the important role business would have within the Ireland of the future. The innovations made at second and third levels of education facilitated the technological demands of business, and equally important, gradually began to change the attitudes of the Irish towards business. The establishment of foreign-owned companies within the country, and the presence of foreign managers living in local communities, also helped in changing these traditional views. The extent of the change that has taken place can be judged from the fact, that in recent years, business related degree and non-degree courses in our colleges are those most sought after by Irish students.

The traditional public image of business was not very high, but then neither was the general calibre of those who were in business. The attitudes and behaviour of many businessmen did not differ much from that of the farmer. They had a small shopkeepers' approach to their enterprise. They were not in any sense entrepreneurial. They had no flair or inclination towards real risk-taking or thinking 'big'. Most were content to take minor, cautious risks, and to add small additions or expansions on to their businesses when this seemed opportune. But the majority of Irish businesses remained family owned and small scale. By the 1930s even Irish industry was still essentially small scale. Businesses were satisfied to serve the home market, and in general had no thought of exporting. Even if they had wanted to export this would have been difficult, since high production costs made their products very uncompetitive. Nor did the adoption by the government of a protectionist policy during the 1930s and 1940s help matters. It merely ensured that Irish industry continued to gear itself to the small, protected home market, and the few large exporting industries which already existed in the country were very unfavourably hit by the protective tariff.

In the absence of any dynamism or initiative from the private sector, evidenced in the lack of private capital, the timidity with regard to expansion and the costs of production which made their goods uncompetitive, the government decided to take action and put a spark into the world of Irish business. They set up, from the 1930s onwards, a number of public companies, whose businesses ranged over a wide field from the Irish Sugar Company to Aer Lingus, to the Irish Life Assurance Company. The emergence of these companies was a major step forward for Irish business. These new companies developed professional managers and managerial approaches to the running of their enterprises. This new breed of businessman, market orientated and professional in his approach, was very different from his conservative predecessor, who was satisfied to operate within a protected market and with little concern for efficiency.

But while there has been much progress in the business area of Irish society, particularly over the last 20-30 years, we still have no room for complacency. Many smaller businesses are still not managed in a fully professional manner. Inefficiencies are still tolerated and passed on to the consumer; there is too little concern with marketing, and with customer relations — the attitude often being that the customer should be grateful for whatever kind of service he gets. Change, and lots of it, is needed in many Irish businesses. But bringing about change in a traditionally-minded society is not the easiest thing to do. Even the warnings regularly given by the government and private agencies, to the effect that businesses which don't change to meet the demands of the Europe of post 1992 won't be around for very long after that, may fall on deaf ears. After all, similar advice, given before Ireland's entry to the EEC in 1973, went unheeded by many businesses, which are, as might be expected, no longer in existence.

All in all it would seem that neither the average Irish farmer or businessman are exemplary models of modern entrepreneurial business people. But then one should not be too surprised by this state of affairs since any thorough study of the Irish reveals that we do not espouse modern capitalist philosophy in a full or total sense. A critical feature of note, when considering economics and the Irish, is the selective way the Irish have picked from modern capitalist thinking the bits or pieces we like, although we do not appear to be committed to many all-important aspects of this philosophy.

An important doctrine of capitalist thinking is that wealth should generate more wealth. Towards this end resources should be used to the maximum and opportunities for expansion should be continuously sought through the development of new products and new markets. This way of thinking and acting is a long way removed from that of the typical Irish farmer who often doesn't even see his land as a resource! It is also distant from the thinking of both the Irish farmer and businessman in relation to new products and markets. Both of these 'entrepreneurs' consider that they have done a good job when they produce something and think that it is the job of someone else — in most cases the government — to find markets for their products. As for developing new products — well, they would seem to have a tendency to become attached to what they are producing and often don't take too kindly to suggestions that new products should be developed in reply to market trends or new technology. I can still see and hear the slightly disbelieving and somewhat irritated response my comment to an agricultural advisor met with in the early 1980s. I suggested to him that perhaps because of the European Community surpluses in milk at the time dairy farmers should be thinking of alternative methods of farming. But he replied 'that's what their land is naturally good for'. It seemed to him to be sacrilegious to even contemplate using it for another enterprise, irrespective of market conditions.

But perhaps an even more glaring and apparent omission in the Irish version of capitalism is risk-taking. The Irish are not generally disposed towards taking risks at all, but if and when they do, they are certainly not prepared to take the consequences that go along with it, in particular the possible negative outcome. This point is continuously being demonstrated by all business sectors in the Irish economy. The company that takes risks and gets into trouble runs like a petulant child to the state demanding assistance. And a few years ago when a large number of farmers got themselves into difficulties, because of the very poor business decisions they made in relation to expanding and borrowing more than they could afford to repay, they ran *en masse* to 'big daddy' the state. They felt very strongly that since things had gone poorly for them they should be bailed out of their predicament. Thus the 'capitalist entrepreneur' in Irish society talks like a capitalist when things are going well for him. But as soon as he begins to experience difficulties he takes on the mantle of the fighter of natural rights. He talks and acts as if one of the fundamental rights within capitalist society is for the capitalist to be rescued by society whenever his risk-taking doesn't come off.

CHAPTER 3

Politics and the Irish

It is almost impossible to understand the Irish unless one recognises and adequately appreciates our political nature. It is without doubt one of our most distinguishing characteristics. Since the early nineteenth century, when our ancestors learned the art of politics and began to engage in it, it has been one of our greatest and most abiding passions.

In addition to discovering that it was something that fires the imagination, our ancestors also found that they had a great aptitude for it. It seemed to come very naturally to them. This talent may have been acquired as a result of their dealings with each other over the centuries, when the activities of bargaining and wheeler-dealing were commonly used in the buying and selling of animals at the local fairs. One could say that perhaps what happened during the nineteenth century was that this talent was developed. The Irish learned the mechanics of politics, the nuts and bolts of it; the tactics and manipulations to engage in, in order to get power.

Our ancestors also learned that they enjoyed not only the getting of power, but the exercise of it as well. Some would say that the power game became something of an obsession with them. Speaking of politics among the Irish in America, one writer has said that it was the power that fascinated them, not the ends which could be achieved through the use of the power. 'Means rather than ends would be their preoccupation. Power for its own sake and for its subsidiary benefits would give them satisfaction.'[1] For the Irish both at home and abroad in America, Australia and the other territories to which they were driven by fear and famine, politics became the master activity.

But the first lesson the student of Irish politics needs to understand is that our interpretation of this activity differs somewhat from the prevailing modern view in terms of both the nature of the activity and how it should be conducted. The version the Irish practice — politics Irish style — is based on our experiences during the nineteenth century. And we have been and continue to be reluctant to change our thinking or actions in relation to an activity for which we have developed so much love and respect. Our liking for the activity is in fact so great, that at times it can seem as if it has taken over our total existence and that the task of living is in fact just one big political exercise. For example, in Irish society politics is often undertaken as a substitute for work and in organisations it can be practised as a substitute for management. In Ireland politics is not just a respected activity, with a great and wide appeal, it is also a very widely used one. However, despite the Irish passion and fascination with politics, it may be comforting and consoling for the foreigner to hear that when it comes to our political system the Irish are responsible and more reasonable and tolerant than might be expected. Since the establishment of the state, Irish society has been at all times a community which has espoused and abided by the principles and practices of political democracy.

Politics Irish Style

The description of politics, outlined in most modern textbooks, is of an activity which takes place between parties with different objectives. The parties engage in bargaining and negotiation, in order to arrive at an outcome where each side involved feels reasonably satisfied. In other words, while each party may not get everything it wanted, it gets enough to make it feel and think of itself as a winner, rather than a loser, in the situation. Certain rules or codes of conduct have developed in relation to the conduct of this activity. For example, it is considered desirable that as many as possible of the parties with an interest in the particular matter, or issue, in dispute, should participate in the decision-making process with respect to it. Participation and involvement are thought to be important elements in the exercise of politics. Also it is generally regarded that since the purpose of engaging in politics in the first place is to amicably resolve differences between sides with different interests and objectives, it is important that all encounters between the parties should not be seen in competitive terms. No winners or losers should emerge. In order to ensure that this doesn't happen, compromise is thought to be very essential. Give and take on the part of all is viewed as being very necessary if the desired win-win outcome is to be brought about. These and the other rules and codes, that have evolved over time, reflect the basic nature of the activity as it is seen in most western societies today. The general view is that it is a civilised way of resolving differences and disagreements between parties of reasonably equal power.

Now the Irish didn't learn their politics in such a civilised or gentlemanly setting. As our ancestors would express it themselves, 'they learned politics the hard way'. The setting in which they found themselves was a dangerous one, requiring devious methods in order to survive, and the kind of politics they learned was closer to the Machiavellian type, where the main concern was with the acquisition, retention and use of power.

Their teacher was Daniel O'Connell a lawyer, who as an Irish Catholic, suffered from many of the restrictions on Catholics which were still in force at the beginning of the nineteenth century. One such restriction was that a Catholic could not be elected as an MP to the parliament at Westminster. In order to agitate to get to this law changed — a necessary step on the way to improving the lot of the Catholics — O'Connell organised the rural peasants into a political force. He set up the first modern political party and party machine. He taught the native Irish how to use the machine in order to gain power and influence over people. He taught them the importance of public meetings, of making rousing speeches, and how to get the vote out. They were quick learners and they soon appreciated what was necessary in order to build up influence and power. And having won Catholic Emancipation from the British government in 1829, they very readily accepted that this was the way to get results — they became 'hooked' on politics.

From these initial exercises at politics, our Irish ancestors developed their own idea or version of politics which went something like this. The first step or stage in politics is to build up a power base through the use of different manipulative tactics, persuasive or otherwise. It is important to ensure that in any situation in which you need to exercise power, you will have enough of it, so it is necessary to work hard at building it up. When one reaches the critical stage of entering the arena with one's competitor, it is important to have enough power in order to win. There is no doubt about what the objective is — it is to win, to get everything you were looking for.

As can be seen from this, the differences between the modern western view of politics and that of the Irish are quite significant. The outcome desired as a result of engaging in politics is different, as indeed are the attitudes and behaviour considered appropriate when partaking in such activities. And even when the same behaviour is used, it is used in a different way, or within a different context. Persuasive tactics, normally used in the modern democratic type of bargaining, in order to achieve a mutually acceptable outcome in a given situation, are used in traditional Irish politics to 'gather in' enough power or influence in order to win.

The interesting point of note is that an observation of the Irish today will show that we still retain the basics of our original view or understanding of politics. We still see bargaining or negotiating encounters in competitive terms, where the objective is to win. And we can show extremely bad grace when in our own terms we 'lose' in these situations, in other words when we don't get everything we are looking for. Nowhere is this attitude more clearly demonstrated than in our dealings with our European Community partners. The ordinary Irish citizen can show feelings of extreme annoyance, frustration and disappointment with the relevant public officials when they arrive back from Brussels without having received everything that was sought there. Claims by an official that he got the best deal he could, that of course he had to listen to the position of the other countries, and compromise in order to meet their needs, don't generally calm the emotions of the citizens. We normally continue to feel let down by the official, who in our eyes, didn't have enough clout to go in there and get what he wanted. Compromise smacks of weakness. It is a demonstration that you didn't have enough power to win, or else didn't use the power you had properly.

If there is one thing that the average Irish person continues to be very conscious of, and knowledgeable about, it is power. We are very aware of our own small degree of influence or power, and how to make the best use of it, or get the most out of it in any situation. So as citizens we are very aware of our vote and how the promise of our own and perhaps our family's vote at the next election can bring pressure to bear on the local politician, so that he in turn will use his political power to intercede on our behalf, in order to get some service or other. We are also likely to see that the best way of getting what we want, in other areas of life, is also by using our small power base to activate larger power-houses, for example, the trade unions in relation to our employment and work relations. The important factor as we see it, is to have a big enough power on our side in any bargaining situation so that we get or win what we want. Research has shown that the Irish are less likely to engage in co-operative activities with other citizens in order to put pressure on people within the political system to do something or other, than citizens in many other democracies. Possible reasons for this behaviour put forward by researchers include, the likelihood that we are not very enthusiastic about the idea of working with other people; another is that we haven't got the skills necessary for group or teamwork. But researchers also suggest that a very likely cause is our general lack of enthusiasm for participation as such.[2] We are not likely to see any great merit or virtue in it unless it gets us what we want. And perhaps we consider that we exercise greater power, and have a better chance of achieving our ends, by going through our political representatives. The real issue is influence, power and getting what you want, not the worth or desirability of participation in the wider context of its value in a democratic society.

It is generally difficult to work out the reasons for the attitudes and behaviour of a group of people, and this is so in relation to the Irish and our tendency to see politics in win-lose terms and to be reluctant to accept compromise. As has been mentioned in another chapter the peasant background, beliefs and values of the Irish may have contributed to our particular view of politics. We cannot easily see or accept the possibility of everyone winning in a situation, since our historical experience, based on circumstances of scarcity, showed what one person gets, another loses.

It is also interesting to speculate on whether our inclination to be non-compromising is linked in any way to the success the Catholic Church had in the last century, when it succeeded in getting us to become more orthodox in relation to Catholic beliefs and practices. Traditionally, we have not been a dogmatic people either in terms of our beliefs, attitudes or behaviour. Historians tell us that even after our conversion to Christianity we still retained what they describe as an Indo-European philosophy to life and living. Christian philosophy, influenced by Hebraism and Greek philosophy very early in its history, came to regard its truth as unique and definitive. It took a dogmatic attitude towards its beliefs and practices. The Christian was obliged to believe and practice those and nothing else. Now it seems that the Indo-European philosophy was much less dogmatic and more tolerant of other beliefs and practices. Consequently, when the Irish converted to Christianity we saw no reason why we had to confine ourselves totally to Christian beliefs and practices. We considered it possible to hold on to elements of our old pagan religion and at the same time be Christians. Alfred Nutt, a writer on the Celts, comments on the retention by the Irish of the spirits from their old pagan religion. He sums up our attitudes and behaviour by saying that 'when dealing with powers so capricious as those of nature, the wise man accepts all the help he can get, the saint may fail here, the fairy there, the witch in the third case, and where one fails the other may succeed'.[3] We obviously believed that we benefited from having two religions from which to draw inspiration and protection.

It is possible that by becoming better Catholics we lost our traditional tolerance. We began to accept that there was a good and a bad, a right and a wrong in beliefs and in situations generally. We started to see things in terms of clean-cut norms, in which there was no scope for compromise. After all, a misdemeanour couldn't be half a sin, it was either a sin or it wasn't. We may have started by seeing and accepting religious matters in those terms. But, gradually, it may have become common and normal for us to bring this way of seeing things to areas and issues outside the religious field. We became more unwilling to compromise and more inclined to want to impose our views on others. 'The acceptability of imposing on others, things one believes to be good and right' was an attitude researchers found in relation to Irish political culture — for example, they found that there was a willingness among the Irish studied to curb political groups who abuse freedom of speech.[4] As in so many other aspects of our character and personality, our contact with western beliefs and attitudes, whether through our colonial experiences, or the Christian religion, may have indeed affected us. And, unfortunately, these influences may not always have been for the better.

Politics — a Substitute for Work

The Protestant Ethic included the belief that hard work was good for the soul and helped one to get to Heaven. It also

included the conviction that it would bring material benefits
here on this earth to all those who engaged in it. It was
however never a view which made any impact on the Irish.
But then they had very good reasons for not seeing any
logical connection between hard work and material achievement or advancement. Under the system of land tenure in
Ireland in the nineteenth century, hard work could have
negative rather than positive outcomes for the Irish tenant.
The tenant who worked hard, who improved the land and
maybe his house, could find that not only was he not compen-
sated for the improvements he had made, but that his labours
were used against him. As a result of his efforts the landlord
might decide that because of the improved state and worth
of his holding he now should pay a higher rent. So much
for nineteenth century landlord motivation strategies!

The Irish peasant knew there was no way he could win
in an economic game of life that was so stacked against
him. So not unreasonably he didn't put much effort into his
material or economic life other than to eke out whatever
meagre existence he could. But as he began to appreciate
the possibilities of what could be achieved using political
tactics, his objective developed into one of changing the
nature and rules of the existing economic game which always
caused him to be the loser. Using politics he was determined
to devise a game which would give him the advantage.

Some say that because agitating and politicking in relation
to land matters paid off reasonably well during the latter
part of the nineteenth and early twentieth century, the Irish
developed an attitude that relates accomplishment and
achievement directly to politics. They associated, and many
would say, we continue to see or relate, material success,
not to work but to politics. One writer has put it this way:
'A cluster of historically conditioned reflexes continues to
influence (the Irish) work ethic. From the Land Acts to the
Common Agricultural Policy many farmers have reaped a
higher return from investment in politics than investment
in agriculture.'[5] Stories from the past depict the traditional

Irish farmer as someone who placed great importance on luck, and on his own bargaining skill at the fair to help him get a good price for his cattle. These ingredients were considered to be far more critical than any hard work which might have been put into the rearing of cattle. His descendant, the modern Irish farmer, holds a view which is not in many cases too different from his forefathers. The only significant difference between the two situations is that now the critical bargaining takes place in Brussels or Dublin, rather than at the local fair.

The Irish attitude to work is often misunderstood and viewed as laziness. But this is not the case at all. The Irish person may work very hard, it's just that he has a different idea or interpretation of what constitutes productive effort. The Irish farmer, busy rounding up support among his fellow farmers, in order to put pressure on the minister to get some act or other changed in Brussels, may in his view be better employed, engaged in politicking, than his Danish or German fellow farmers, busy working in their fields. The following hypothetical picture sums up the situation, as seen from the typical Irish perspective. The Danish and German farmers are busy in their fields taking the weeds out of their crops. But the Irish farmer is busy trying to use his contacts to get some merchant to buy his crops with the weeds in them, or else he is lobbying his parliamentary representative to get Brussels to pay as much for crops with weeds as weed-free ones. And if he succeeds in his efforts then won't he be as successful in the final outcome as his European colleagues!

It would be unfair however to imply that it is only the farmer who tends to substitute politics for work. The industrial worker also reacts in this way. By putting a lot of effort into politicking and getting things well set up for himself he can overcome the need to have to break his back at work. A strong union can ensure limited access to a trade or craft, it can dictate the demarcation lines between himself and others, it can tell the employers what they can and can't ask him to do. In other words, it can ensure that the results expected of him are not, as he sees it, too demanding.

Politics — a Substitute for Management

'We (the Irish) are not a nation of managers — we are a nation of fixers', so says one commentator and he probably has made a very good and valid point.[6] The term 'fixer' is used by the Irish to describe someone who is constantly engaged in politicking.

The traditional Irish manager, in other words the manager who has not been trained to think or act in what would now be considered a professional managerial manner, normally sees politicking as the primary and essential ingredient in management. He considers that it is vital for his success to have lots of contacts. Towards this end he spends a lot of time and effort discovering the right people to get to know, and actually getting to know them. In addition to developing a good network of contacts, he also likes to be able to do favours for people so that he can seek return favours if and when this becomes necessary.

Most professional managers would see nothing wrong with the behaviour of our traditional manager up to this point. All managers recognise the importance of good contacts. The problem is that the traditional manager sees this as the beginning and end of the job. He spends his time putting himself in a powerful position, but why? Well, he normally has no clear-cut objectives or targets that he wants to achieve, no plan to work to, and consequently no proper basis for control. Unlike the professional manager who wants power to achieve specific things, the traditional manager wants power for no clearly specified purposes. Of course he aims to make himself as powerful as possible and to do well in his business but what exactly 'well' is, is not normally clarified.

In the absence of good management the traditional manager creates more problems and difficulties for himself than would the good professional manager. For example, because of poor planning in relation to the transport of goods to a valuable customer, he may find that all the hauliers are busy and he can't get transport to deliver his goods. He now has to fix the situation by using some of his contacts to overcome the problem. He pulls in a favour from someone. At the end of the episode he may consider, and even boast, about the way he managed to deal with the situation. In his own eyes he showed himself to be a superb manager — he had the necessary contact or pull to overcome the difficulty, he used it and solved the problem. It may not be apparent to him that the whole affair demonstrates extremely poor management, since good planning would have avoided the problem in the first instance. In non-profit organisations, managers of course don't have to be concerned with economic survival and so can engage in, and enjoy, politics as an end in itself. They are free to acquire and use power to enhance their own positions within the organisation without having to worry about using it for economic survival purposes.

It is probably true to say that many Irish organisations, both private and public, would be much better, more successful, effective and efficient if the 'fixer' management style gave way to a professional management style. If, in other words, some of the politics could be taken out of them.

Politics in the Political System

All actors in the Irish political system, whether seeking to get power, or exercising it, operate in a manner that is for the most part, reasonable and restrained. Politicians do not engage in Tammany Hall-style politics, for which the Irish became famous in the United States. Pressure groups do not resort to unduly violent or offensive tactics when seeking to have their cases heard in the public arena. Nor do citizens engage in bribery or corruption when seeking services from public servants.

In all these situations the range of activities and actions considered acceptable and legitimate have evolved over the years, and they do not include any actions or behaviour that would be unacceptable in other western democracies. Verbal truculence, marches, demonstrations and even withholding of taxes are all acceptable, when used by individuals or groups in an effort to get their point of view across, and get the government to pursue a certain course of action. But activities designed to hurt individuals or groups are not tolerated, for example, cutting off vital food supplies, or intimidation. Politicians are free to pursue the full range of persuasive tactics when trying to win over the public and get their vote. But the more flamboyant tactics of the old style Irish politics are not acceptable, and the days of buying votes, in the literal sense, are well and truly over. It seems that all in all the Irish are much restrained and austere in public morality at home, than we are traditionally reputed to have been in the United States and elsewhere!

When engaging in politicking within the public or political sphere, interest groups generally act responsibly. While in many cases they put up a good fight to win their cause, when beaten and forced to compromise on an issue they normally give in and accept the agreed position. There are of course noticeable exceptions, instances when groups refuse to go along with the decision of the government, and continue to protest and disregard the law in an obvious and deliberate manner. The more normal situation is for groups to accept, at least overtly, the new law or governmental decision. This does not mean of course that they will necessarily obey the law, or go along with the policy decisions. For, as has been mentioned in a previous chapter, we Irish are not renowned for our adherence to laws, which each Irish person sees as being there for everyone else to obey but not himself! In Irish society the real difficulty is normally not getting laws onto the statute books, but having them enforced. Some critics maintain that if the Irish had half the number of laws we have at present, but enforced these effectively, Irish society would be much better governed and managed than it is at present.

CHAPTER 4

The Irish Mind

The Irish have traditionally been seen as a people with a deeply spiritual mind, and many would say that we still maintain this spiritual way of looking at life. For example, an Irish person when walking past an old castle is likely to sense or feel the presence of the old mediaeval occupants in a very real way. So in describing the Irish as spiritual I mean that we do not confine our existence, and that which we think is real, to what exists in the physical world. We acknowledge the existence of other worlds, or more specifically other forms of consciousness, outside the ordinary day-to-day consciousness. These other realms — spiritual worlds — are just as real as the ordinary everyday physical world. Neil Jordan, one of our modern writers and film makers, describes this characteristic of the Irish very well when he says that, 'the attempt to imagine another state of living, another way of being is, I believe, very Irish. It's something to do with the quest for another place and another manner of thinking. It's a dissatisfaction with the accepted and scientifically approved explanations of the universe.'[1]

The Irish, in holding this spiritual philosophy of existence, are not of course different from many other groups of people, both primitive or modern. After all, all people who adhere to a formal religion are asked to accept the existence of a world outside the ordinary material one. What distinguishes the Irish is the nature of our spiritual realms, their composition in other words, the intensity of the feelings of love and fondness which we have for these worlds, and the sustained influence these worlds have exercised over our life down through the centuries. It often seems that the Irish are happier in imaginary worlds than in the real material world. Many would say that the realms of fiction and imagination are much more to our liking than the world of fact and reasoned analysis. Perhaps this may help explain another distinguishing feature of the Irish mind — its non-intellectualism.

The Irish as a group are not much given to thought — or to the process of thinking and reasoning our way through an issue. Our natural predisposition is to leave well enough alone, and to operate on the basis of established doctrine and past experience. But if forced to think anew about a situation or issue, the way we arrive at our conclusion or decision — the mechanics of our thinking and reasoning processes — may seem strange to the foreigner. This would be particularly the case for those who have been brought up and encouraged to have a thoughtful and very rigorous analytical approach to arriving at a conclusion and/or making a decision.

This latter feature, our lack of interest in reasoned thinking, which demonstrates itself in a lack of interest in ideas, philosophies, etc., and our lack of skill in relation to this kind of thinking could be seen as reducing the benefit or usefulness of the other two features. We are good at using our creative imaginative powers, but we may not get as much value from this very positive attribute as we should or could. The imagination can come up with a vision or a dream, but it needs a good thinking mind to take it beyond the stage of a vague notion in the mind, to give it substance which would enable it to be pursued as a dream or vision which is to become a reality. The development of the thinking part of the Irish mind would make it a mighty powerful one.

The Spiritual and Creative Mind

The practice of setting up spiritual worlds outside the ordinary world of day-to-day consciousness has been fairly common among mankind right through history. People in all parts of the earth have come up with their own gods, heavens and hells. Modern secular man is more the exception than the rule when he closes off the possibility of the existence of realms outside the ordinary material one, maintaining that it is the only true world that really exists and all others are purely imaginary. In addition he considers that all those who enter these worlds are suspect mentally. Sigmund Freud, the great psychologist, put forward modern man's position on this subject when he maintained that the inner world of dreams, visions, myths, etc., were nothing more than the human subconscious trying to cope with difficulties in the external life of the human. The existence of an inner or spiritual world was seen as an unhealthy sign in the individual — a sign that he had a need for a psychoanalyst. But while intellectuals, such as Freud and Marx, consciously and openly renounced the world of the spirit, many ordinary individuals merely drift into a totally materialist existence that places little or no importance on the spiritual. It often just happens that, bit by bit, reality outside the material world ceases to have any meaning or relevance. Of course this can happen even though they may still practice a religion. Being a member of a Church, attending to the ceremonies and rituals of a religion or adhering to a religious code of morality, does not necessarily indicate a spiritual person. It does not denote an individual for whom the life of the spirit has any real meaning or significance.

But what of the Irish today? After twenty years or more of intensive exposure to the materialist culture of western societies, what is the spiritual health of the Irish mind now? To what extent do the Irish remain a spiritual people? There is a good amount of evidence around to suggest that we appear to be holding out fairly well. We continue to remain a fairly religious people, at least, if the statistics are to be believed. For example, over 90 per cent of the Catholic population still attend Mass at least once a week. And while, as has been said, this does not in itself prove that this number are spiritual in any real sense, nonetheless it is probably reasonable to conclude that a good percentage of those attending Mass experience some degree of spirituality in their lives.

In addition, in our ordinary day-to-day existence many Irish still demonstrate the importance that a spiritual life has for us. God and the heavenly spheres never seem to be very far away — 'if it's God's will', 'I'll say a prayer for you', 'God bless you...'. Figures from the heavenly world are constantly being called on to offer assistance to those in need. Even the young, the least committed believers, of whom it was discovered that over 25 per cent had forsaken their religion, take a cautious view when it comes to jettisoning the spiritual as opposed to institutionalised religion — even the possibility of ghosts is not totally rejected out of hand by most of them.

But perhaps the strongest case for thinking that the Irish are still probably a spiritual people is our history. Even a surface study of the Irish and our spiritual existence down through the centuries would lead the student to conclude that it is likely to take longer than 20-30 years of materialist philosophy to erode worlds that have been such an integral part of our lives for so long, and about which we have shown such strong feelings.

The first important point to make in relation to our history is that following the Reformation which started in the sixteenth century, the Irish remained Catholic, so consequently the Irish mind remained a Catholic mind. It continued to live in the rich spiritual world of mediaeval Catholicism, which was full of heavenly visions of angels, devils and demons. It was a world rich in symbols and images — a Michelangelo kind of world that suited the personality of the Irish since it provided our ancestors with the rich material they needed to feed their fertile imaginations. Historians tells us that the Celts, the ancestors of the Irish, were a highly imaginative people and their descendants seem to have the same characteristic. In addition to drawing on

Catholicism for spiritual sustenance the Irish continued also to call forth the spirits of the old pagan world — the banshees, fairies, etc. Thus there was abundant material available from which to draw inspiration.

The spiritual worlds of our ancestors were rich and very real to them. Jesus, Mary, the saints, ghosts and fairies, were as real as were the material objects in their day-to-day existence. Stories, poetry and language reveal this fact, even the simplest greeting in Irish. Hello — *Dia 'gus Mhuire dhuit*, translates as God and Mary be with you. Every second word was frequently an invocation to someone within the heavenly sphere. The following short extract from *An Old Woman's Reflections* by Peig Sayers, a typical traditional Irish story, shows the closeness of the heavenly world to the physical one — 'The great sea was coming on top of us and the strong force of the wind helping it. We had but to send our prayer sincerely to God that nobody would be taken sick or ill. We had our own charge of that because there wasn't a priest or doctor near us without going across the little strait and the little strait was up to three miles in length. But God was in favour with us, eternal praise to Him. For with my memory nobody died without the priest in winter-time.'[2]

Our ancestors' spiritual worlds fuelled their imagination, or perhaps it was because of their imaginative disposition that they were exceptionally spiritual. It is difficult to work out which came first. What appears certain however, is that the two characteristics supported each other. Their imagination, working on the rich spiritual realms they had created, provided them with a reality that was breathtakingly large. One writer in referring to it has said that it was so large it was difficult to get the English language to fit it. Language seemed to be inadequate to deal with it. So he speculates that this predicament may have caused the Irish to develop a fascination with language, and to consider that they had to engage in a constant and continuous reworking of it, so that it might handle better the vastness of the existence that presented itself.

It is interesting to speculate on the effect a change to some of the Protestant religions might have had on the Irish mind. One thing is certain, the Irish mind with its great need for imaginative sustenance would have found many of the more austere Protestant religions very cold and spartan. A religion based on cold doctrines and without rich imagery and symbols would probably have had very little appeal. Our ancestors' attachment to the Catholic religion was never in doubt. They fought and suffered for it, and like all people who fight for a cause, the more they fought for it, the more important and precious it became to them. Indeed, it became a very essential part of their existence. The very fight or struggle itself — the persecutions they endured in seeking to hold on to it — became, in turn, further fuel for their imagination. Images of the Catholic Irish, reduced to the condition of poverty-stricken peasants, sheltering on cold, barren hills while on the run from British soldiers because of their religion, are described and depicted in vivid form in Irish poetry and stories.

Not only have the Irish lived in a very rich spiritual world from which they have derived much that has made life bearable for them, but they have lived with this as an essential part of their existence. Unlike many societies in Europe, Irish society did not experience the social and cultural turmoil that resulted from the coming of the age of science, technology and industrialisation. While gradually over the course of the nineteenth century, traditional culture gave way to modern culture in many parts of Europe and North America, Irish society and culture remained relatively untouched. The old spiritual way of seeing the universe and of seeing man within that universe remained relatively unchanged until very recently. God rather than science was seen as the source of all knowledge and He provided all the explanations in relation to the creation and maintenance of the universe. While eager to enjoy the benefits which new advances in science and technology brought, e.g. the railway and new industrial machinery, a healthy doubt was retained about all the progress that was going on in the world. Our ancestors didn't always share the great confidence of modern man in science and what it could do. In fact one sometimes gets the impression, in reading their writings, that deep down they were often wondering what God was thinking in relation to the changes man was seeking to make on world order.

Certainly, the absence of an industrial revolution in Irish society enabled the Irish to maintain their strong spiritual life right into the twentieth century. The industrial revolution, when and where it occurred, resulted in bringing about conditions and a whole philosophy and way of life that was very unfavourable to the spiritual life of people. The physical conditions within which the human had to live and work were often soul destroying and certainly dampening for the imagination. In many instances the individual lost his dignity as a human being, and was treated as a kind of human machine — something that only had a material presence with no spirit or soul. The writers of the Romantic School and critics of Victorian society in England, were in no doubt as to what was happening in industrial society. Man, they felt, was losing his spiritual dimension — 'men are growing mechanical in head and heart, as well as in hand'.[3]

However, in Irish society the individual retained his full humanity. His soul or spirit, that which made him different from other creatures, was always fully appreciated. The Irish continued to have a holistic view of life. We didn't confine ourselves to simply seeing or stressing one particular part or dimension of our being. Rather we saw ourselves as a unified whole — a creature with both a body and spirit. In the Irish view of life, the worth or dignity due a person was never directly related to his material position, to wealth or to the kind of work done. It was believed that the individual was due dignity and respect simply by being a human and thus made in the image and likeness of Christ.

The individual in the Irish view of life was never seen as a machine whose prime purpose was to work. In contrast to a philosophy which saw the main reason for man's existence as work and the gratification of physical needs, the philosophy of the Irish was that the prime purpose of life, other than getting to heaven, was living. Consequently for the Irish time had to be given to living, to doing the things that were judged important and critical. So enjoying oneself, telling stories, talking with ones friends, and many other activities, were considered important. From a material viewpoint these activities could be regarded as worthless. But from the Irish point of view they were thought to be of the highest importance and essential if one was to live life to the full. And the Irish philosophy of life and living hasn't changed much over the years. The person is still seen as a creature of God, with both a body and soul, who may aim eventually to get to heaven, but in the meantime, with God's blessing, would like to enjoy living here on earth!

If one believed in impersonal forces one would say that history has been conspiring to keep the Irish mind spiritual and imaginative. Neither the Reformation of the sixteenth century, nor industrial revolution of the nineteenth century were allowed to interfere and possibly make significant changes in these two features. The final stage in this 'plot' could be seen as having taken place in the 1960s. Just as Irish society was beginning to come more under the influence of modern materialist thinking and values, these very ideas and values themselves began to be questioned within industrialised societies. In America, writers such as Charles Reich and Alvin Toffler, in their books *The Greening of America* and *Future Shock*, questioned the old values and consciousness of modern society and considered that a cultural revolution was needed if man was to continue to survive on this planet.

This questioning may have caused the more thoughtful Irish person to take heed and consider just how 'modern' Irish society should become. The ordinary Irish person wasn't too caught up in these kinds of questions however, and was busy trying to make up for lost time. The develop-ment of the consumer society and the availability of all those nice material things was beginning to make it difficult to have the interest in, or time for, things of the spirit. Although busily trying to catch up and become as materialistic as the next, the Irish still haven't quite got there yet, and 'hopefully we never will' is the view and sentiment expressed by many within our society.

Many Irish are aware of the worst effects of materialism, alienated individuals with no real sense of meaning or purpose in life, individuals who are 'uptight' and so busy that they have no time to switch off and to just relax or dream. But while knowing the possible negative consequences of materialism some are still drawn to it. As other societies are trying to bring back the life of the spirit, and help the individual to regain the power to dream, the Irish are running the risk of losing these qualities which traditionally we have had. The battle to keep the Irish mind spiritual and imaginative is being fought out at present, and while it is difficult to predict the outcome, our natural disposition and traditional regard for these qualities gives ground for hope.

Non-Intellectual

The Irish have great respect for the story-teller — the person who can hold a group in awe by virtue of his powers of imagination and language. The wit and poet are also very acceptable. They can even take and sometimes enjoy the rhetoric of the politician with his big words, use of emotional language and store of other psychological ploys. The one person found difficult to accept is the man of reasoned thought. Well-thought-out and reasoned discourse, ideas and philosophy are just not for us.

Our feelings, in listening to a reasoned debate on a subject, would include boredom and frustration. The niceties of the speaker's logic, the sophistication of his concepts or ideas would all be lost on us. Our feelings might extend to ones of annoyance and even dislike — the reason being, we just don't like intellectuals. We get lost in their arguments, and don't know half the time 'what the hell they're going on about at all!' Instead the Irish love practising the manipulative thinking required in politicking, the imaginative thinking required in telling a story or joke, but we have no liking at all for logical thinking and no interest in practising it. All of this, of course, begs the question, why? — why do we enjoy all language games other than this one?

A strong possible explanation is that, traditionally, we have never placed the intellect or reasoning faculty of our species on a pedestal. We never elevated it or downgraded the other human faculties, as groups more influenced by Graeco-Roman culture did. For us, the senses, imagination and feelings have always been accepted as at least as important.

The work of the old Irish Christian monks from the sixth to the twelfth centuries, demonstrates this point very well. These men of the highest learning wrote down the old Celtic legends and stories that had been passed on orally up to then. But, despite the very early introduction by them of a written culture in Irish, these monks retained and perfected the features of an oral tradition. They concentrated on the use of narrative and imagery in their work rather than progress on to develop an abstract language which would have made it possible for them to engage in analytical reasoning. They did not follow the pattern of Greek men of learning, such as Plato and Aristotle, in this respect. It therefore seems that unlike the Greeks, when given a choice between telling stories about the past or engaging in speculative reasoning, the Irish chose the former — preferring and perfecting the imagination over the intellect.

It would appear that we are a people who find it difficult to let the reason have the long rein it is often given by groups more influenced by western thinking. Such people are often quite happy, in fact prefer in many cases, to let their intellect loose to tackle tasks on its own, leaving the remainder of their faculties free to take a holiday. In contrast, the Irish person is more inclined to bring all his faculties to work on the job to hand. It has been argued that it is this inclination and capacity that contributes to our success in literature and writing generally. When engaged in writing a book, we do not throw out our senses, feelings and imagination so that the intellect can write the book without distraction. Instead, the various faculties are called on to assist and support each other. Imagination may be called in to help abstract thought and all the time the senses may be busy monitoring what is going on and offering suggestions in relation to the rhythm, the words, the flow.

We Irish don't place undue reliance on the intellect. But even when we do use it, some writers have maintained, most notably Richard Kearney in his book *The Irish Mind*,[4] that we reason our way through a problem or issue in a slightly different method to the traditional western way. We are told that the Irish mind never came under the influence of the reasoning logic of the Graeco-Roman culture which dominated most of Western Europe and that, as a result, we never picked up this 'way of thinking'. A critical feature in the Graeco-Roman reasoning logic was the division or the separation of opposites, A was A and B was B, and A couldn't be B. So things were either one thing or another, they couldn't be both. In the Irish way of thinking things were not divided up, so consequently things were not seen in terms of opposites, so A could be B. In other words, things could be seen in two ways at the same time. So in the Irish mind something could be both good and bad at the same time, while in the classical way it could only be either good or bad. Thus the Irish find it difficult to divide things into separate and discreet opposites. As we see it, there are bits of good in even the worst people or situations and, likewise, traces of bad in even the best.

The reader may find it difficult to accept that as a people we remained so removed from traditional western thinking. After all, what about the influence of the Catholic Church? A significant feature here is that the Irish Church over the centuries remained relatively isolated from the mainstream of European thinking and influence. It developed as a Church that was never much given to intellectual endeavours. Speculation on the great issues that engaged continental thinkers had little importance for the Irish Church. It is interesting to note that it had no intellectual centre until 1795 when Maynooth College was set up, and we are told that this institution did not put much importance on the intellectual or cultural development of its priests. What was wanted was a simple unquestioning faith. The novel *Father Ralph*, written in the 1890s, gives an insight into the culture of the college.[5] Ralph finds theological speculation of any kind dismissed by professors and students alike — any opinion contradictory to the accepted one brings the angry reply 'that what is good enough for St Thomas and me ought to satisfy you'.

Perhaps it is not surprising, therefore, that priests who were brought up and educated not to ask questions, but to accept the ideas and doctrines given to them without question, would in turn adopt a similar attitude in their dealings with lay people. The Irish Catholic was taught to accept what God and his bishops and priests told him, and that was the end of the matter. The idea conveyed was that the truth was known and therefore reasoned thinking or discussion on it was inappropriate, since it implied that there might in fact be another version of it.

Additionally, our contact with the English over the centuries didn't assist us much in terms of developing a rational and analytical approach to matters. In their handling of public issues and in their administration of public bodies, they showed themselves to be as disinclined to engage in thinking and rational analysis as we are now in our public bodies. The reality is, that we don't engage in as much intellectual discussion or rational analysis as we should. In places where one would expect to find a lot of lively intellectual discussion and analysis taking place, such as in public service bodies, one might be surprised to discover just how little was actually taking place.

The observer of Irish public organisations can at times get the impression that if a government minister asked a senior civil servant to come up with a new policy on a specific issue, the civil servant would proceed to give it to him on the spot — off the top of his head, so to speak. The need for, and the requirements of, good well-reasoned thinking and analysis just don't appear to be seen or appreciated by a lot of Irish people. And if the civil servant was asked, as part of his policy development exercise, to develop and indicate a clearly stated philosophy on the issue — he would probably consider that the minister had gone a little strange in the head. After all what has philosophy got to do with administering a government service! But then, the hypothetical situation outlined here is likely to remain academic, since it probably would be quite unusual for any government minister to be looking for such airy-fairy things as philosophies and in-depth analyses of issues. He might be branded an intellectual if he behaved in that manner, and as one political scientist said, 'one of the dirtiest words in Irish politics (and Irish life) is intellectual'.[6] If the priest is generally positioned at the top of the status chart in Irish society, the intellectual is certainly close to the bottom of this table.

We need to get over this hang-up we have about the intellect and rational thinking and analysis. We also need to develop thinking and analytical skills in our people to a greater extent than we have up to now. In particular, we need to train our young people. The Irish educational system would never have been seen as one that encouraged independent thought or thinking. And while it obviously has changed in many respects over the years, the extent to which it encourages independent thinking in students, even at present, is open to question. In too many cases the student is still more likely to be given and expected to use the notes of the expert or the teacher, when critically commenting on a subject or topic, rather than required to think and analyse the subject for himself. Critics of the educational system often maintain that the system produces 'parrots' rather than thinkers. It helps its students to develop the skills of memory or recall but not the skills of reasoned thinking, where the student has to logically reason his way from the premise of his argument all the way through to its conclusion.

There are, of course, definite weaknesses in the traditional western elevation of the intellect over the other human faculties, and in western-style reasoning. Thus we Irish need to appreciate the benefits we have traditionally derived from seeing and doing things our own way. But for day-to-day living and surviving in a complex world, we need to accept the importance of using our intellect more than we do, and of engaging in more regular and frequent rational analysis of problems and situations.

CHAPTER 5

The Irish at Work — Where We Fall Down

Every visitor has some kind of contact with the Irish in a work capacity, whether it is as a customer in a hotel or tourist office, or working with us in a business relationship. So a knowledge of what we're like at work may help in dealing with us. In addition it may also further the visitor's general understanding of us as a people.

The first critical point to make is that in a modern world dominated by organisations the Irish are not good or effective organisation people. This situation is the prime cause or source of our great difficulties and problems in relation to survival in the modern world. Our natural qualities or characteristics do not equip us well for coping effectively in an organisation-orientated and dominated world. In fact the qualities and characteristics needed for effective functioning within organisations appear to be very unnatural and alien to us. Many years spent trying to train people in organisational management has led me to the conclusion that management is basically foreign to the Irish. We appear to have no natural aptitude or flair for it. The Irish are not naturally results-or task-orientated. The thinking and analytical disposition necessary to set objectives, targets and plans; the natural discipline and organisation required for effective and efficient functioning within organisations, are too often almost totally absent in the Irish person. In addition the high degree of alertness and responsiveness to change needed in the modern organisation is also often missing in Irish workers and managers. Nor does the fact that we are unable to co-operate with each other on a group or team basis improve this overall bleak situation.

The modern Irish organisation can easily delude the observer into thinking that it is modern in a true managerial sense. It may have all the trappings and surface appearances of modernity — modern technology may be in evidence, modern ideas may be spouted, modern systems may even be in place. But very often underneath all, the essentials or substance of real management may be missing — results, discipline and co-operation may be ideas to be talked about rather than deeply held and internalised beliefs and behaviour.

Many aspects of our traditional philosophy, thinking and way of life are at variance with modern management thinking and behaviour. Our traditional philosophy is not sufficiently one-dimensional for management purposes. It stresses aspects of life other than the achievement of material objectives and ends; it places importance on the enjoyment and living of life rather than discipline and work itself; it emphasises the importance of seeing the person as a human being rather than primarily a consumer or human resource. In general the Irish live very happily with this traditional philosophy of life and living. The difficulty is that we also have to live or survive economically in the modern world. Consequently we have a need to balance these two sets of values — our traditional values and management values — and this we haven't yet satisfactorily achieved. The first stage in the solving of this balancing problem may be a recognition by us that we actually have a problem in relation to management. The first requirement may be to accept that in general our natural disposition within organisations is to muddle through rather than manage. However, the difficulty is that we are unlikely to face this reality. We are likely to fall down in relation to the very first requirement of good management — facing reality and accepting when something appears to be going wrong.

Discipline and Organisation

We Irish have a tendency to take our liking for disorder, rather than order, into the workplace, and the normal or average Irish organisation would rarely be noted for its crisp military-like discipline or orderliness. One senses in the case of organisations where people have been trained or socialised into operating in a well-disciplined and ordered manner that it is very much a learned or acquired behaviour. And with our natural disposition kept under control we often remind one of people who have been stuffed into tight boxes, or starched clothes, and who show signs that we eagerly await being released and set free, at the end of a day's work.

In no area do we Irish show our lack of discipline to a greater extent than in relation to time. We seem to find it enormously difficult to have our lives ruled by clocks and schedules. Trying to get the Irish to be on time, or to adhere to schedules is a frustrating, almost soul-destroying exercise. It is important to state of course, that we are not the only group of people for whom work discipline is difficult. As one writer on attitudes to work in different cultures put it, 'a disciplined attitude towards work is not only not common in many cultures, but in most it is specifically deplored'.[1] He goes on to say that these cultures emphasise the search for satisfactions in life which often are destroyed by the discipline adhered to in some modern industrialised societies. It is considered that even in the workplace there should be time to enjoy the company of others, to talk longer than might be required by the specific task to hand, etc.

It would probably take enormous numbers of psychologists, anthropologists and other specialists to work out why the Irish are so totally lacking in discipline in relation to time — but it is important for the foreigner to know that we are undisciplined. If a meeting or gathering is scheduled to start at 9.30 a.m. some of the participants will inevitably arrive after the set time. Their excuses, if they even feel that such is warranted, will be that they got held up in traffic, etc. Of course if they were organised they would have allowed for possible delays and built in a certain amount of contingency time into their schedule. The fact is that the Irish just don't take time too seriously. An arranged time is an approximate rather than definite time, so what difference does a few minutes make one way or the other! Time in many cases is not seen as a limited resource and the old Irish attitude which maintains that 'when God made time, he made lots of it' still prevails.

This failure to see time as a limited resource manifests itself in many different ways within Irish organisations, apart from an inability to be on time. For instance, it shows itself in a general disregard for time management in relation to meetings. These gatherings often have no planned finishing times, and enormous amounts of time are regularly wasted at them. It is difficult to know whether trying to get the Irish to see time as a limited resource would make us any better at using it efficiently and effectively. But of course even if a manager succeeded in achieving this in his own company he could still expect to operate in a general environment in which time is disregarded.

It often happens that it is when disagreements or grievances arise between the workers and management within an organisation or company that the Irish show their lawless or undisciplined leanings in their fullest and most lethal forms. There is nothing peculiarly Irish about the fact that problems arise between workers and management. This happens in all societies, but the Irish views, attitudes and behaviour in relation to the resolution of these difficulties can too often become disorderly and undisciplined. Even though a framework of procedures is laid down and institutions are available to solve problems or disagreements, the Irish worker will think nothing of throwing aside all of these formalised ways and doing things his own way. If matters are not going his way within the formal structures and procedures, then his attitude may be 'to hell with them' and he'll proceed to take the situation into his own hands. The Irish worker doesn't necessarily see himself as bound by the formal rules, nor even indeed by his union. And the unofficial or wildcat strike is not an unknown feature in Irish industrial life. It seems that the line between abiding by the rules and doing things your own way is often very thin in the case of the Irish worker. Nor is it unknown for union leaders to have the view that it is not their role to discipline and manage workers. While not condoning the actions of individuals or groups who go against them, they don't always give an outright condemnation or rejection of their behaviour.

It is important to say, however, that the level or degree of disorder and disruption which results from actions such as unofficial strikes is not very high in Irish organisations. The biggest problems the manager is likely to have to deal with are the numerous minor levels of disorder which result from poor organisation. Poor organisation of work and resources, such as time, can be seen at all levels within the typical Irish company unless staff training and development has reduced or eliminated it.

The lack of organisation and method which the typical Irish worker demonstrates in carrying out his tasks is often difficult to believe. Take the example of the workman who arrives to carry out certain repairs to the house or to an appliance. He normally arrives later than the scheduled time. He almost invariably discovers on his arrival that something hasn't been provided for, for example he hasn't taken certain critical tools or materials with him, so he has to return to his base to pick these up. When he arrives back and surveys more closely the work to be carried out, there is a good chance that he will decide that he needs some colleague or other to help him with it, so he has to make arrangements with him, and wait for his arrival. By the time he is ready to go to work, there is a good chance that the working-day is over, so the actual work may have to be carried out on overtime rates.

But it is not only the Irish worker whose work effectiveness and efficiency is reduced significantly by poor organisation. The Irish manager often shows the same tendencies. The typical Irish manager has improved a lot in recent years in relation to the basic organisation or scheduling of his time — diaries and other more sophisticated work planners are now very much in evidence. But despite appearances, the manager is often poorly organised in relation to the actual carrying out of his tasks. To take one example, his conduct of a meeting — too often Irish meetings resemble what might be called happenings. In other words they are spontaneous get togethers which have no clearly defined purpose. It is not unusual for the participants to have been inadequately briefed on the purpose of the meeting. A vague agenda may have been sent to them, but it is likely it didn't adequately inform them about the nature of the business to be undertaken, whether an issue was merely to be discussed or a decision taken with respect to it. As for the chairing or management of meetings themselves — the lack of organisation is often enough to make one feel dizzy. Issues and points seem to arrive from nowhere — are tossed around and abandoned, only to reappear after a respectable period of time and so they go round again, and again, and again...! The meeting generally ends when everyone seems to have had enough of it, or when other commitments — lunch appointments etc. force it to come to a hasty end. And the exhausted participant is often left in a state of bewilderment, trying to work out what, if anything, was decided, and what action, if any, he or anybody else has to take as a result of the meetings!

If the picture presented here seems too bad to be believable, unfortunately it is not. Poor organisation of tasks and activities results in an enormous amount of wasted time and effort in many Irish companies and organisations.

Win-Lose Attitudes

The Irish predisposition to see all those around us as potential enemies, and to regard situations of disagreement or conflict in win-lose competitive terms, also finds its way into Irish organisational life. It is certainly undesirable that in any encounter the Irish person is inclined to regard the other individual as an enemy. But it's nothing short of disasterous for the well-being of his organisation if, in addition, the view is held that the only way to deal with this 'enemy' is by defeating him every time. The tendency to see others within the organisation as threats or enemies is not unique to the Irish. There is more than enough research available to show that this competitive attitude exists in many organisational cultures, outside Ireland. However the problem takes on added dimensions of seriousness within the Irish situation. The general failure of the Irish to accept compromises when negotiating or bargaining adds a very dangerous element to these situations.

The dynamics that normally occur in win-lose confrontations are commonly seen in Irish companies.They can be observed in the dealings between groups within organisations and in union-management negotiations. Each party starts out with an attitude of winning. As it gradually becomes apparent that the other is not going to give in to its total demands, each side begins to take up an entrenched position. The likelihood then is that the encounter begins to become nasty or dirty. The longer the contest continues, the more attitudes deteriorate and the more determined each party becomes to win at any cost. Wider objectives, such as the well-being of the company or society can often be lost sight of and appear secondary to the primary objective of bringing the other party to their knees.

This feature of the gradual deterioration in communication and relations between parties, which results when negotiations take place for an extended period of time without reaching a mutually satisfactory outcome has been noted and commented on in the field of Irish industrial relations. It has been observed that the longer a strike goes on in Irish society the more difficult it will be to resolve. Each party is more likely to dig in its heels with increased determination and prepare itself for a long siege ahead. Ethics and even common sense are often abandoned as each side prepares to fight to the end. As one eminent commentator on the Irish industrial relations scene has said: 'It is almost as if men were determined rightly or wrongly to win their point of view, the only limit being the extent of their power to inflict damage on society or the company.'[2]

There does not appear to be any doubt that the Irish view of the world which is based on rather primitive assumptions is undesirable in both a modern civilised society and in a modern effective organisation. Greater training in team-work and increased opportunity to work on a team basis may help the situation. One of the reasons that has been put forward for the inability of the Irish to function well in a co-operative manner with others is our lack of group or team skills. This has been attributed in some measure to the limited opportunity the young Irish person has to gain practice in group skills, because of the dearth of extra-curricular activities in Irish schools. It is to be hoped that increased competence in teamwork will result in the ordinary Irish worker and manager seeing the necessity for effective co-operation with others, in order to achieve their own and their companies objectives.

Not Enough Concern with Getting Results

The Irish worker considers that if he puts in the required number of hours in his workplace then he has fulfilled his obligation to his employer. If he works hard in carrying out his tasks during that period then he feels he has more than fulfilled his obligations. What he actually achieves or accomplishes during his hours on the job, and as a result of his hard work, is rarely of concern to him. He considers that he gets paid for the work he does, not for his success in achieving specific results. In fact the worker would probably think that attempts to impose standards or targets on him are outside the range of his obligations to his employer.

But as in the case of many other work characteristics, it isn't only the Irish worker who lacks a natural concern with getting results. The Irish manager also shows the same inclination. The Irish manager's objective is too often just to keep the show on the road — to keep the business going, or in the situation of the public service manager to maintain the old in-basket and out-basket under control! Neither manager is very inclined to think beyond the day-to-day activities. They are unlikely to seek answers to such fundamental questions as — what is all the activity taking place in aid of? what do we want to achieve through it? or as a result of it? Thinking ahead and deciding on the goals and targets they want to meet and setting out to meet them is a very unnatural way for Irish managers to operate. And since operating in this way is in essence what modern management is all about, it could be said that in general management just doesn't come naturally to Irish managers.

This lack of interest in getting results is widely suspected and often publicly commented on. One ex-government minister, Justin Keating, put the matter bluntly in 1988 when he stated that 'a lot of our cock-ups in business have occurred because of the total refusal of managers to think strategically.'[3] When he asked Irish companies, who were going to be critically affected by Ireland's entry into the EEC in 1973, what they would like as a defence strategy, he was told that they were fine as they were. It was obvious to the minister that they hadn't thought ahead and adequately considered the implications of Ireland's entry into the EEC. Consequently they hadn't formulated any strategy for dealing with this event, and it is not surprising to discover that many of these companies are no longer in existence. However it seems that Irish managers still haven't learned the lessons of the dire consequences of not thinking strategically. The ex-minister is still very apprehensive about the extent to which Irish managers are planning for the introduction of the single European market in 1992.

The same inertia in relation to forward thinking and planning is found in managers within the public sector. A former Taoiseach painted a very vivid picture of this passivity when he described civil servants, as hanging around 'waiting for new ideas to walk in through the door'.[4] Efforts to change this situation were made during the 1970s. Attempts were made to set up a system that would get managers to think ahead and decide on objectives for their departments and set policies and programmes in line with these objectives. But despite much time and effort being devoted to the exercise, it never took off, and the comments of many seasoned bureaucrats at the time that this new system just wasn't on were proven correct.

Thus it seems that in the public, as in the private sector, managers spend a lot of their time mopping up disasters which have taken place as a result of their poor management. Both groups of managers have a strong tendency to sit back and wait for things to happen before they take action. Even after training many managers still find it difficult to make the running in their areas of operation. They continue to have a reactive approach to problems and issues, and are constantly forced to catch up with others — either competitors from other countries or local groups who are screaming for action.

The general Irish characteristic of taking things as they come rather than planning for, and bringing about the changes you want, seems to be very deeply imbedded. And it would appear that a lot of re-education still has to be carried out in order to get Irish workers and managers to acknowledge the crucial importance of results within an organisation.

Too Little Analysis

The Irish manager's attitude and behaviour in relation to adopting a thoughtful and analytical approach to problems and situations is in sharp contrast with his managerial colleagues from other cultures.

The typical French or German manager tackles problems full of 'Cartesian' fervour. He places, as one writer has said, 'great stress and emphasis on extended intellectual effort and precise planning as a prelude to action'.[5] He digs deep into the problem or situation like a little animal burrowing. He sifts and sorts all the stones along the way, assembles these into little piles, labels and analyses them thoroughly. He hopes that at the end of his efforts he will have a comprehensive understanding of the problem and what he should do about it. However he often runs the risk of losing himself in the holes. He can get so caught up with the complexities of his study, with the multitude of stones of different sizes, shapes and origin, that he loses sight of the purpose of his digging in the first place.

The American manager is generally much more tempered in his analytical efforts. While he places great importance on analysis, he is less inclined to go as deeply or thoroughly into the problem or situation as his European colleagues. He digs into the problem, identifies the few critical rocks or bigger stones and from these draws his conclusions and makes his decision.

The typical Irish manager on the other hand is likely to do no digging at all! In fact he is probably unaware of the tools available to help in the digging exercise. The Irish manager just doesn't appear to see the use or advantage of engaging in rigorous analysis of a problem or situation. When presented with a problem he likes to make his decision right away on an instinctive or intuitive basis. He dislikes delays and can become quite frustrated with the long period of inactivity which analysis entails. Anyway he doesn't think that he would get a return for such an investment of time and effort. It would indeed be very demanding for him, for he often lacks the basic skills required for good analysis. Even managers with good professional qualifications appear in many instances, to be unable to carry over into their managerial jobs the basic thinking skills which they learned in their professional training. The average manager when asked to carry out a piece of analysis shows many basic weaknesses. He is unable to handle ideas or concepts and often treats these as if they were words to be defined rather than concepts to be explored and analysed. The complexities associated with the analysis of concepts are often totally strange to him and he is frequently out of place in studying them, like a fish out of water in fact.

Nor does he fare much better when required to think and reason his way through a piece of analysis. It is easy to lose him when moving from one level of thinking to another. He finds it hard to gradually progress in a logical fashion from one level to another. And when a group of managers are working together on a study this deficiency creates enormous difficulties. Group work and efforts often become extremely complicated and confusing. The Irish manager carrying out an analysis often resembles an explorer operating without a map, constantly wondering where he is and where he should go from there.

While it may not be generally appreciated by him, there are many negative consequences arising from his failure to appreciate the importance of good analysis and his inability to carry out this activity effectively. The most serious consequence is his inability to develop new ideas. The manager can only develop new policies and strategies for his organisation, through study of his own unique situation. Without doing this he is confined to making minor incremental changes to what he is doing at present, or else copying the example of another company. He cannot, however, invent for himself really new and different ways of going about things.

Some commentators have said that Irish organisations have suffered because of a shortage of new ideas. One critic in discussing the public service has said that in recent years efforts have indeed been made to put in place the structures necessary for thinking. Unfortunately he also says that 'these have not been accompanied by increased thoughtfulness in the evolution of new policies and effective plans'.

This may also be the case in the private sector — a consequence not only of a passive attitude towards the future, but also of our inability to develop good ideas that are specifically geared to a particular company and its future.

CHAPTER 6

The Irish At Work — What We've Got Going For Us

We Irish are not, however, without our redeeming features as workers and managers. A perusal of the last chapter might lead the reader to conclude that there is no hope for us — that we just haven't got what it takes to make good workers or managers. In terms of organisation and rationality we are definitely poor. But these aren't the only qualities required within business and public service bodies and in more recent years these very features or qualities have come under review and criticism by many experts in this field.

Peters' and Waterman's book *In Search of Excellence*, one of the most quoted works of this decade, renders many heavy blows to the 'Gods of Rationality' who reign supreme in the overly ordered and rational organisations of the 1980s.[1] In their view an over reliance on order and rationality is causing many companies to suffocate themselves, to lose their creative capacity and their ability to respond effectively to their customers' needs. Over-emphasis on rational qualities has, in their opinion, led to an imbalance in management. Critical features such as creativity and the ability to implement plans, to get things done, have too often taken second place within the modern business company.

So everything is not yet lost for the Irish — for our strengths lie in these two areas. We have the potential for creativity — the very disorder of our minds which makes organisation and rationality difficult for us, offers the potential for great creativity. Our political sensitivity, the innate sense of knowing and understanding power, is a strong point when it comes to getting things done within an organisation. Knowing the right people to approach and how to deal with them are certainly desirable attributes and skills for the manager to have. When this quality is combined with a generally affable disposition and natural ability to relate well to people of all types it provides the necessary temperament to deal with staff, customers and business colleagues.

A Capacity for Creativity

The Irish mind is one in which imagination and intuition rather than reason and logic dominate. Even education and training seem to be unable to reverse this natural inclination. It is not to say that we Irish are without value in the work-place. A simple visualisation of the differences between the two kinds of mind at work — the rational and the creative — may help the reader to see the potential benefits the Irish mind can offer the business world.

Let us look first at the rational mind. Everything in it is in nicely organised boxes, labelled and categorised, nothing is out of place. New ideas or experiences are assessed and if accepted are directed into their appropriate boxes or files. Only selected ideas and experiences are let in. The consequence of all this selection and tidiness is that potentially useful ideas and experiences are often screened out.

Now to the creative mind, in which ideas and experiences lie around all over the place. They are generally not filed away, and if filed at all it is possible that they are placed in boxes with unrelated ideas or experiences. Thus the outcome could be the coming together of two unrelated ideas, for example, a metaphor from a piece of poetry and a scientific idea. The result of this fusion might be the creation of a new poem, a new scientific theory or some other form of innovation.

It is easy to see from this little visualisation the Irish person's great natural capacity for creativity. In his mind it is relatively easy for disassociated ideas to come together. And as Arthur Koestler has said when discussing the creative

mind, 'the conscious and unconscious processes underlying creativity are essentially combinatorial activities —
the bringing together of previously separate areas of knowledge and experience'[2] — a process which is automatic for
most Irish people. This ability to create new ideas, new
ways of looking at things, is evident even in our day-to-day
living. It shows in the freshness of our humour and wit,
usually devoid of cliches or repetition. The figurative
language we use also very often demonstrates a high
degree of creativity. The average Irish person has a capacity
for coming up with the most bizarre images and metaphors,
that bring together the most unlikely things or events, but
which in their composition demonstrate a high level of
creativity.

The Irish manager shows this same tendency towards
creativity on training courses. The one area where he doesn't
really need training is in relation to creative problem
solving, or brainstorming, as it is called in management
circles. In a creative problem solving exercise the manager
is asked to suspend judgement, and off the top of his head
indicate all the multitude of ways a particular problem
could be seen and defined, and the numerous solutions that
could be adopted to solve it. The typical Irish manager
takes to this exercise like a duck to water — it presents no
problem to him. He can fill a whole room with ideas in a
few minutes. And he probably wonders after all that creativity
why he is not allowed to brainstorm all the problems he is
presented with on the course. It would be preferable to
having to wearily plod his way through them, using an
analytical approach!

However, whether this innate capacity for creativity and
innovation is developed and used in the workplace is, of
course, another matter. Features such as the individual's
motivation and the culture of the organisation will have a
large bearing on whether this natural talent is used or not.
One of the most noteworthy and regrettable features of
Irish public organisations in the past has been the contrast

between the culture of inertia which existed within these bodies and the extraordinary life, vitality and creativity of many who worked in these organisations. So many of our greatest men of letters have been civil servants who were allowed to contribute none of their enormous amounts of creativity to the betterment of the public service.

We are a society with lots of creative talent, with lots of potential for innovation, but will it be used? It is well for all our managers to remember that successful companies, according to Peters and Waterman, are those 'that make sure that the potential innovator comes forward, grows and flourishes, even to the extent of indulging a little madness.'[3] In organisational thinking in the last few years, it appears that the creative capability of the individual is a feature very highly regarded and sought after within companies that are at present prospering, and who hope to remain in that enviable position in the future.

Political Sensitivity

The Irish person is a natural political animal, and he takes his innate sense and instinct for power and politics into his organisational life. His 'map' of any organisation includes not just the formal arrangements of authority and responsibilities but also the network of power and power relationships within the company. He knows only too well that things are not always as they appear on the surface and that the individual with a fancy title, high profile and lots of the trappings of power might, in fact, when studied more closely have in reality very little muscle and consequently be of little use to him. Incidentally such an individual would be described by the Irish as all show — in other words, he only has the appearance of power. This type of person is generally not found to be very attractive to the Irish. We dislike showy things or show-offs at the best of times, and particularly when individuals have nothing behind them to back up their image. We hold the view that the image projected by the really powerful is understated, since those with real power do not generally want others to know just how powerful they are or they might become targets for the envy and hostility of others. This latter point is particularly relevant in Irish society where those who have made it big are likely to suffer from the jealous and spiteful feelings and comments of begrudgers.

The 'power map' which the Irish individual develops in relation to a company or organisation has many uses. The most obvious is that it helps him in his dealings with individuals within the company. He knows where decisions are really made and who the critical actors are. But equally important it can be his starting point in relation to increasing or enhancing his own power and power base. As a result he must also be aware of the vagaries of power and the constant need to keep up to date with the ebb and flow of power within an organisation. Thus they appreciate that there is a requirement for regular briefings and discussions with colleagues to find out how things are going on this front. Regular chats over a beer are an excellent way of getting an update on the power chart. Casual comments such as 'I heard that things are not going so well for X, they say he's on the way down', may be the opening line in a conversation, the purpose of which is to find whether there has been a shift of power, and if so, who seems to be winning or losing. The individual seeking to further his own position uses this knowledge to identify those he should get to know, or know better, and for whom he might be able to be of assistance in some way. The more favours he can carry out the better. Not only is it good for the ego to have others indebted to you but it also means that you can call in favours if and when needed. When the manager needs to get the staff to work overtime it certainly helps if he can get on to the foreman for whom he has done a good turn, and ask him if he would now do him a favour.

There is always the danger with the Irish person that he may become too concerned with politicking so that it becomes a substitute for work or management. However the manager who sees management without politics is probably more of a liability. The individual worker or manager who thinks and believes that organisations operate as rational entities according to formally laid down rules and procedures, etc., and who doesn't look beyond these formal features, probably finds it difficult to function effectively in any organisation. It is unlikely however that the average Irish worker or manager starts out with a rational view or model of an organisation. He begins, rather, with a political one. As he sees it organisations are places where different people have different degrees of power and the extent to which they can achieve success in what they want to do is very much determined by the amount of power they have. Using this as a basis, training courses have been developed in Ireland to get managers to move on and develop objectives and strategies that are in line with client or customer needs.

The Irish characteristic of seeing power as the critical and essential force in the social world, as energy is in the natural world, and our ability to understand and deal with it is, in general terms, a positive and desirable work and organisational quality. The individual worker or manager who takes this feature with him into the organisation is bringing with him a quality which is very difficult to teach to people. It is much easier to teach an individual rational problem solving, communication, or interpersonal skills than to instill in him an instinct for power and how to handle or manage it in any specific situation.

Affable Disposition

When structuring this book I decided that it was appropriate, and even proper, to keep the strongest card of the Irish until last — our warmth and friendliness. These are the characteristics for which we are probably most renowned. Our affability seems to contain a special degree of attractiveness, perhaps because what we project towards people are genuine feelings. They are not learned phrases delivered in a mechanical fashion and designed just to be nice to the customer or colleague. When dealing with people the Irish are very conscious of the fact that we are dealing with human beings who have feelings, anxieties and sensitivities.

The importance of sensitivity towards people, as people, is a very critical element in Irish culture. We are extremely careful, and very reluctant, to do anything that would hurt people's feelings, offend them, or cause them embarrassment in any way. This extreme sensitivity gives rise to a number of features in our behaviour that often confuse the foreigner. The Irish often take very round-about routes when approaching certain issues, particularly delicate or sensitive matters which could result in unpleasantness for some of the individuals involved. Cases in point are when we have to give bad news, criticise or discipline someone. In these types of circumstances we never tackle the main issue straight on, as it were, but go around it, hoping that by coming at it gradually and gently, it will hurt or offend less. An excellent example of this softly softly approach is portrayed in one of Frank O'Connor's stories.[4] He tells of a policeman calling at a mountain farmhouse to collect a small fine imposed by the court on an old man for a minor offence. When he had climbed up the mountain he greeted the old man as if he had no reason for calling to see him, other than to enquire about his state of health and wellbeing. He stayed for tea and just as he was about to take his leave he paused and asked, 'I don't suppose you'd be thinking of paying that wee biteen of a fine they put on you a while back'. The story shows the sensitive and courtly manner in which the policeman handled the situation. The visit was made into a social occasion, with the official purpose assigned a lesser importance. The old man's feelings were considered to be more important than simple efficiency, which would have required just going to the door and asking him for the fine.

Of course, this concern with not hurting or causing distress to others can have negative implications, particularly in organisational life. Many Irish managers have a tendency to procrastinate and put off tackling difficult or potentially nasty situations, such as disciplining staff, because they are apprehensive about the possibility of offending the staff member involved. Their dislike of dealing with these types of cases is such, that they are often prepared to do anything, even allow the state of affairs to deteriorate, rather than risk causing themselves and the other people involved distress and unpleasantness.

We Irish are not only indirect in our way of handling certain types of situations, we also tend to be very indirect in our communication. This characteristic is often very bewildering to the foreigner, who may come from a society in which people say simply and directly what they want to say rather than beat around the bush as the Irish are inclined to do. The story that is often told to demonstrate this tendency is that of the tourist who asks an Irishman whether he is on the right road to Cork or wherever. The Irishman fails to give a direct answer but confuses the tourist by his long answer, which indirectly tells him that he's not on the right road, but is not very far away from a road that would take him there. A straightforward blunt no seems unfriendly, almost hurtful to give, so the natural inclination of the Irishman is to soften the blow as it were, by telling him that everything is not lost and he's not far away from the road he wants. In a similar way the subordinate who asks his boss how he's doing, will never get a direct reply — particularly if his work isn't up to scratch!

Directness and bluntness in communication are definitely not Irish characteristics. In fact the Irish find it difficult to relate to people who behave in this way. To us they seem very hard, harsh, ungracious and discourteous. If an Irish individual asked a salesperson whether he had a particular item in stock, and the reply was a direct 'Sorry we haven't, we'll have it on Saturday', the customer would feel entitled to a more gracious reply. This could be an explanation as to why they didn't have the item, or even an expression of hope on the part of the salesperson that the customer would be able to come back to get it on the Saturday.

Our longwindedness or blarney, our convoluted communication, often makes it difficult for the foreigner to understand us. But this is not generally caused by a desire to delay people, or place greater demands on them than is necessary. Rather, it results from a simple desire on our part to ensure that in each encounter with a human being that person is treated in a manner befitting a human being. We Irish like our society to be this way and it is the quality we miss most when away from Ireland. Indeed it is these qualities of warmth and friendliness which the foreigner generally likes most about us. In fact, they forgive us a lot because of them. Our tendency to be disorderly, not sufficiently task-or results-orientated, at times not very rational — these and many other characteristics are often, at least partly, forgotten and forgiven because of the genuine human glow we exude. In an electronic age perhaps foreigners also like to feel that there are still some really 'human' humans around.

Notes

Chapter One

1 Matthew Arnold, 'Lectures and Essays in Criticism', as quoted by F.S.L. Lyons in *Culture and Anarchy in Ireland 1890-1939*, p.5, Oxford, 1982.
2 Patrick O'Donnell, *The Irish Faction Fighters of the Nineteenth Century*, Dublin, 1969.
3 Sir Henry D. Ingliss, *Ireland in 1834*, as quoted in *The Irish Faction Fighters*, p.10.
4 Walter Bryan, *The Improbable Irish*, p.145, New York, 1969.
5 Tom Garvin, 'Change and the Political System', from *Unequal Achievements — The Irish Experience 1957-1982*, edited by Frank Litton, p.33, Dublin, 1982.
6 Basil Chubb, *The Government and Politics of Ireland*, p.240, London, 1982.
7 Declan Kilberd, lecture at Yeats Summer School, 1986.
8 Seán Ó Tuama, *The Gaelic League Idea*, as quoted by Desmond Fennell in *The State of the Nation — Ireland since the Sixties*, p.125, Dublin, 1983.

Chapter Two

1 George Foster, 'Peasant Society and the Image of the Limited Good' as quoted in J. Raven, C.T. Whelan et al., *Irish Political Culture*, p.53, Dublin, 1976.
2 'Irish Adults' Perceptions of Civic Institutions' in Raven, Whelan et al., *Irish Political Culture*, pp.56-59.
3 T.J. Barrington, 'Whatever Happened to Irish Government', from *Unequal Achievements*, p.105.
4 Terence Brown, *Ireland — A Social and Cultural History 1922-1985*, p.156, London 1987.
5 Ibid., p.157.
6 Ibid., p.157.
7 F.S.L. Lyons, *Culture and Anarchy in Ireland 1890-1939*, p.8.
8 Thomas Davis, 'The National Language', from Arthur Griffith, *Thomas Davis — The Thinker and Teacher*, p.55, Dublin, 1914.
9 Douglas Hyde, 'The Necessity for De-anglicising Ireland', as quoted in F.S.L. Lyons, *Culture and Anarchy in Ireland*, p.42.
10 Terence Brown, *Ireland — A Social and Cultural History*, p.135f.
11 Francis Stuart, 'Things to Live for' as quoted by F.S.L. Lyons in *Culture and Anarchy in Ireland*, p.171.
12 Charles McCarthy, *The Decade of Upheaval — Irish Trade Unions in the Sixties*, p.9, Dublin, 1973.
13 F.S.L. Lyons, *Ireland since the Famine*, p.608, London, 1985.
14 Quote attributed to Michael Shanks by Martin J. Wiener in *English Culture and the Decline of the Industrial Spirit 1850-1980*, p.139, Middlesex 1985.

Chapter Three

1 Thomas N. Brown, *Irish–American Nationalism 1870-1980*, p.179, Philadelphia and New York, 1966.
2 Raven, Whelan et al., *Irish Political Culture*, p.51-54.
3 Alfred Nutt, 'The Celtic Doctrine of Rebirth II', chapter XVIII, p. 204, in Kuno Meyer and Alfred Nutt, *The Voyage of Bran and Celtic Doctrine of Rebirth*, London, 1897.
4 Raven, Whelan et al., *Irish Political Culture*, pp. 51-54.
5 Joseph Lee, 'Society and Culture', from *Unequal Achievements*, p.10.
6. Alec Wrafter in the *Cork Examiner*, 1 May 1982, as quoted by Joseph Lee in 'Society and Culture', in *Unequal Achievements*, p.10.

Chapter Four

1 Neil Jordan in *Across the Fontiers — Ireland in the 1990s*, edited by Richard Kearney, p.198, Dublin, 1988.
2 Peig Sayers, *An Old Woman's Reflections*, pp130f., Oxford, 1987.
3 Quotation from the works of Thomas Carlyle as given by Raymond Williams in *Culture and Society 1780-1950*, p.86, Middlesex, 1982.
4 Richard Kearney, *The Irish Mind, Exploring Intellectual Traditions*, p.9, Dublin, 1985.
5 Gerald O'Donovan, *Father Ralph*, London, 1913.
6 Quoted by Basil Chubb in *Government and Politics of Ireland*, p.57, attributed to a lecture by Proinsias Mac Aonghusa, reported in *The Irish Times*, 20 January 1967.

Chapter Five

1 John Fayerweather, 'Personal Relations', from *Culture and Management*, edited by Theodore Weinshall, p.128, Middlesex, 1977.
2 Charles MacCarthy, *The Decade of Upheaval*, p.17.
3 Justin Keating, *Management*, Vol. 35, No. 3, p.3, March 1988.

4 Sean Lemass, 'The Organisation Behind the Economic Programme', from *Administration*, Vol. IX, p.5, 1961.
5 John Fayerweather, 'Personal Relations', p.127.
6 T.J. Barrington, 'Whatever Happened to Irish Government', from *Unequal Achievements*, p.99.
Chapter Six
1 T.J. Peters and R.W. Waterman Jr., *In Search of Excellence — Lessons from America's Best-Run Companies*, New York, 1982.
2 Arthur Koestler 'The Creative Mind', from his work *Janus — A Summing Up*, p.129, London, 1979.
3 Peters and Waterman, *In Search of Excellence*, p.202.
4 Frank O'Connor, 'The Majesty of the Law', from *The Oxford Book of Irish Short Stories*, Oxford and New York, 1989.

Select Bibliography

General History:
De Paor, Liam (ed): Milestones in Irish History, Thomas Davis Lecture Series, RTE/Mercier Press, Cork & Dublin, 1986.
Kee, Robert, *Ireland — A History*, Abacus, London, 1982.
Lyons, F.S.L., *Ireland since the Famine*, Fontana, London, 1985.
Matthews, Caitlin, *The Elements of the Celtic Tradition*, Element Books, Dorset, 1989.
Moody, T.W. and Martin, F.X., (eds), *The Course of Irish History*, The Mercier Press, Cork & Dublin 1976, Revised Edition 1984.
O'Brien, Maire and Conor Cruise, *A Concise History of Ireland*, Thames and Hudson, London 1985.
Raftery, Joseph (ed.), *The Celts*, Thomas Davis Lecture Series, RTE/The Mercier Press, Cork & Dublin, 1988.

Culture and Society:
Brown, Terence, *Ireland — A Social and Cultural History 1922-1985*, Fontana, London, 1987.
Connell, K.H., *Irish Peasant Society*, Clarendon Press, Oxford, 1968.
Connolly, Séan, *Religion and Society in Nineteenth Century Ireland* (Studies in Irish Economic and Social History 3), The Economic and Social History Society of Ireland, 1985.
Danaher, Kevin, *In Ireland Long Ago*, The Mercier Press, Cork & Dublin, 1962.
Deane, Seamus, *Celtic Revivals. Essays in Modern Irish Literature 1880-1980*, Faber & Faber, London, 1985.
Kirby, Peadar, *Has Ireland a Future?* The Mercier Press, Cork & Dublin 1988
Lee, J.J., *Ireland 1912-1985. Politics and Society*, Cambridge University Press, Cambridge, 1989.
Lyons, F.S.L., *Culture and Anarchy in Ireland 1890-1939*, Oxford University Press, Oxford & New York, 1982.
O'Brien, Jack, *British Brutality in Ireland*, The Mercier Press, Cork & Dublin 1989.
Whyte, J.H., *Church & State in Modern Ireland 1923-1979*, Gill and Macmillan, Dublin, 1980.

Government and Politics:
Barrington, T.J., *The Irish Administrative System*, I.P.A., Dublin, 1980.
Boland, Kevin, *Under Contract with The Enemy*, The Mercier Press, Cork & Dublin 1988.
Chubb, Basil, *The Government and Politics of Ireland*, Longman, London, 1982.

Language:
Ó Donnchadha, Diarmuid, *The Irish Phrase Book*, Bord Na Gaeilge/The Mercier Press, 1986.
O'Farrell, P., *How the Irish speak English*, The Mercier Press, Cork & Dublin, 1980.
Joyce, P.W., *English as we speak it in Ireland*, Wolfhound Press, Dublin, 1988.

Work and Organisation:
McCarthy, Charles, *The Decade of Upheaval — Irish Trade Unions in the Sixties*. I.P.A., Dublin, 1973.
Administration, journal of the Institute of Public Administration of Ireland (published quarterly).
Management, the official magazine of the Irish Management Institute (published monthly).